Medieval Kingdoms

THE YOUNG OXFORD HISTORY OF
BRITAIN & IRELAND

Medieval Kingdoms

Alfred the Great ~ Henry VII

JOHN GILLINGHAM

General Editor
PROFESSOR KENNETH O. MORGAN

OXFORD
UNIVERSITY PRESS

OXFORD
UNIVERSITY PRESS

Great Clarendon Street, Oxford OX2 6DP

Oxford University Press is a department of the University of Oxford.
It furthers the University's objective of excellence in research, scholarship,
and education by publishing worldwide in

Oxford New York

Athens Auckland Bangkok Bogotá Buenos Aires
Cape Town Chennai Dar es Salaam Delhi Florence Hong Kong Istanbul
Karachi Kolkata Kuala Lumpur Madrid Melbourne Mexico City Mumbai
Nairobi Paris São Paulo Shanghai Singapore Taipei Tokyo Toronto Warsaw

with associated companies in Berlin Ibadan

Oxford is a registered trade mark of Oxford University Press
in the UK and in certain other countries

Paperback ISBN 0-19-910829-3

1 3 5 7 9 10 8 6 4 2

Designed by Richard Morris, Stonesfield Design
Printed in China by Imago

CONTENTS

❖

CHAPTER 1

The kingdoms in Britain & Ireland

❖

Here, two kings who have just won a battle are shown back in their palace deciding what to do with a valuable prisoner. This picture is taken from an Anglo-Saxon translation of the Book of Genesis *from the Bible, and the prisoner is Lot.*

When the great Viking army landed in 865 there were a large number of separate kingdoms in the British Isles. The four Anglo-Saxon kingdoms were Northumbria, Mercia, East Anglia and Wessex (see map on page 8). There were at least four kings in Wales, one or more kings of the Isle of Man and the Western Isles, several kings in the far north and dozens in Ireland. But by 1066, nearly 200 years later, a dramatic change had taken place in one part of the British Isles. There was only one Anglo-Saxon kingdom: England, a rich kingdom whose borders were already very much like those of England today. Beyond England kings continued to rule their smaller, poorer kingdoms exactly as they had done for centuries. A great contrast had emerged, between a single state in the richer lands of lowland Britain and many smaller and poorer kingships in the north and west. This contrast was to shape British history for many centuries to come. How did it come about? Why did England grow so differently from the rest?

For kings, and men who wanted to be kings, wealth was the key to power. To get power they had to have plenty of followers, and to hold on to them they needed to reward them. How could they become rich enough to do this – and then stay rich enough to keep on doing it? In societies where people's wealth was held mainly in animals and food crops, it was not easy to become rich quickly. For men who were in a hurry the only way was to steal.

So kings and would-be kings spent much of their time raiding each other's lands. What they were after were the most valuable goods they could lay their hands on: precious metals, cattle and slaves. In these raids kings were also, of course, expected to defend their people. Kings who failed might be killed or mutilated. As the fortunes of war swung from one king to another, so kingdoms rose and fell.

A big Viking army attacked the kingdom of Wessex in 871, the year in which Alfred (871–899) became king. After hard fighting Alfred bought time by paying them not to attack, but in 876 and 877 they came back. In January 878 the Danish king Guthrum launched a midwinter attack. Taken by surprise, Alfred fled to the Isle of Athelney in the Somerset marshes. Here he found a safe refuge. He needed one. Vikings were no kinder than other people, and kings who fell into their hands were usually killed or mutilated. In the last few years they had killed King Aella of Northumbria and King Edmund of East Anglia. They had also defeated the Mercians and driven their king into exile. Wessex was the only Anglo-Saxon kingdom which had not been overthrown by Viking attacks.

In 878 many of the people of Wessex, the West Saxons, submitted to the Vikings, but Alfred refused to give up. He summoned an army to meet him at Egbert's Stone and led it to victory at the Battle of Edington. Guthrum was forced to make peace. After this great victory Alfred made new laws, built fortresses and ships, and captured London. When the Vikings attacked again, between 892 and 896, Alfred did not have to flee. His defences held firm. Wessex had survived.

When Alfred took over London he changed his title from 'King of the West-Saxons', to 'King of the English'. He also issued a special coin to commemorate his triumph.

Alfred the Great

Of all English kings Alfred is the only one known as 'the Great'. Yet we know very little about his reign except what we are told in two books: the *Anglo-Saxon Chronicle* and one by a Welshman, Bishop Asser, who wrote a *Life of Alfred*. The writers of both books show Alfred as a great king. The story of the Battle of Edington in 878, of an heroic king who retreated to Athelney in order to fight on when all seemed lost, comes from them. The *Anglo-Saxon Chronicle* was begun in Alfred's reign, probably at the king's command, while Bishop Asser was favoured by Alfred and liked to think of himself as the king's friend. Did these books make Alfred appear greater than he really was? It is difficult to answer this question because we do not have many other documents about him. It is possible that he made sure that the writers of the *Chronicle* and his friend Asser made him appear very courageous and noble, to persuade people to follow him in his battle against the Vikings.

All wise kings knew they had to influence the way people thought about them. They liked to hear singers and storytellers tell of their own deeds, as well as about past heroes. Very few of these songs survive, because in a society where few could read or write the chances of their ever being written down were small. In *Beowulf*, probably written earlier in the eighth century, we can see the system at work. No sooner has Beowulf dealt with the monster, Grendel, than we are told that,

> a man with a gift for words, whose mind was stored with a host of old legends, composed a new song. Juggling with phrases he told the story of Beowulf's exploit, comparing it with the deeds of past heroes.

Alfred's descendants took full advantage of the destruction of the other three ancient English kingdoms by Danish armies in the ninth century.

Alfred had a love of learning and of books which at that time was most unusual. Most kings could neither read nor write – they had others to do that for them. Alfred invited scholars to his court and learned Latin when he was forty. Asser helped him to translate some important Latin books into English; often Alfred added his own ideas to these

This magnificent enamel plaque in an ornate gold frame depicts King Alfred and probably belonged to him. The lettering around the frame says, in old English, 'Alfred had me made'. It was found near Athelney in Somerset, where Alfred hid from the Vikings and where he later built a monastery.

The creation of England

- Norwegian lands in 880
- Danish lands in 880
- Alfred's kingdom of Wessex
- other Saxon kingdoms
- lands conquered by Alfred and his successors by 955

0   50   100   150 km

Kings were also expected to settle quarrels and to act as judges. One letter-writer remembered how Alfred 'in his chamber at Wardour' insisted on finishing washing his hands before he would give a decision in a difficult case. After Alfred's death the case was re-opened, much to the writer's disgust. 'Sir', he wrote in a letter to Alfred's son, King Edward, 'if men wish to change every judgment which King Alfred made, when will we ever stop disputing?'

This eleventh-century picture shows a king holding a staff and the sword of justice, surrounded by his counsellors (the witan). He has just ordered a man to be hanged.

translations. He started a palace school for his leading men (called ealdormen) and their sons. No other king in the whole of English history so stands out from those around him. It would be over 300 years before England had another king who could read and write. Other evidence about Alfred comes from his laws, which were written down, some documents called charters and his will. One law is about blood feuds, that is tit-for-tat fighting between families. Other laws and charters show him trying to see that people, especially the wealthy, were given justice. In his will he rewarded faithful servants and left money for the poor.

Alfred the Good?

This does not mean, of course, that Alfred was necessarily a 'good man' as well as a 'great king' – although he is often pictured in later books as the model of a brave and honest Englishman. A few pieces of evidence suggest that some churchmen thought that he robbed the churches. Although Alfred was generous to some churchmen (to Asser for example), it is likely that he rewarded his soldiers with lands which monks lost control of during the turmoil of the Viking invasions. What else should a king do when fighting for his life, and needing soldiers to fight for him?

Whatever methods Alfred used against the Danes, the fact remains that he succeeded. His kingdom survived the Viking storm and it was on this foundation that his descendants were to build the kingdom of England.

This silver penny was minted in the reign of Edward the Elder. The design probably represents one of the fortifications built by him and his sister, as they conquered the Midlands from the Vikings.

Conquering the Danelaw

By the time Alfred died in 899 he had made his own kingdom safe from Viking attack. It was his children, his son Edward 'the Elder' (king of the West Saxons from 899 to 924) and his daughter Aethelflaed, who really started the triumphant growth of Wessex. By 920 Edward had conquered Danish Mercia and East Anglia, and pushed his northern frontier as far as the Humber river. Edward was a very successful war lord, but his sister Aethelflaed's achievement was even more extraordinary. In that society women usually played only a small part as rulers. Ruling mainly meant fighting, and war was a man's

This is the frontispiece, or opening page, of a manu-script book The Lives of St Cuthbert *(in prose and verse) by Bede. A great (but humble) king offers a book to a saint, whose hand is raised in blessing. When Athelstan conquered Northumbria he visited St Cuthbert's shrine in 934, and gave many gifts to the church there. This precious book was one of those gifts.*

business. Aethelflaed had been married to the English lord of Mercia. When he died in 911 she ruled Mercia for seven years, making the decisions which led to the capture of Derby and Leicester from the Vikings. She had no son of her own, but she brought up her brother's son, Athelstan.

When Edward died, Athelstan (924–939) took over the combined kingdom of Mercia and Wessex. He too was a great general. In 926 he captured York and continued to press forward on both his western and northern frontiers. He was so aggressive that nearly all his neighbours – the Vikings of Dublin, the Scots and the Britons of Strathclyde – allied against him. These allies invaded, but they were defeated in the great Battle of Brunanburh in 937. According to the *Anglo-Saxon Chronicle*,

Copies of the Anglo-Saxon Chronicle *were sent, probably on King Alfred's orders, to various churches throughout his kingdom. In some of these churches, later writers added their own descriptions of events. The result is that several versions of the* Chronicle *still survive today, each one telling a slightly different story.*

In this year King Aethelstan, lord of nobles, dispenser of treasure to his men, and his brother also, Edmund Atheling, won by the sword's edge undying glory in battle around Brunanburh. Never yet in this island before this ... was a greater slaughter of a host made since the Angles and Saxons came hither.

The West Saxons entered the Danelaw as conquerors. When Athelstan died in 939 the Northumbrians would not accept his successor, Edmund (939–946), as king. Instead they asked the Norse Viking king of Dublin, Olaf Guthfrithson, to be king of York. Edmund successfully re-conquered the north, but when he was assassinated, in 946, once again the men of York chose a Norse Viking king, Eric Bloodaxe (947–954), as their ruler. According to the *Anglo-Saxon Chronicle* for 948, 'In this year Eadred [Edmund's brother, the new English king] ravaged all Northumbria because they had accepted Eric as their king'.

Eric Bloodaxe was killed in 954, and once again York fell to the army of Wessex. Gradually the Northumbrians accepted West Saxon rule. When Eadred died in 955 the West Saxons remained in control of York. If any one year marks the foundation of the kingdom of England it is 955.

The new state was still torn by struggles for power. King Eadwig (955–59) faced an opposition party strong enough to set up his very young brother Edgar as king in Mercia. When Eadwig died in 959 England was swiftly re-unified under King Edgar (959–975) who, in 973, was crowned 'Emperor' in Bath. The ruins of the Roman city must have reminded people of the earlier Roman Empire. The new English kingdom was clearly now the strongest in the British Isles – while it remained united.

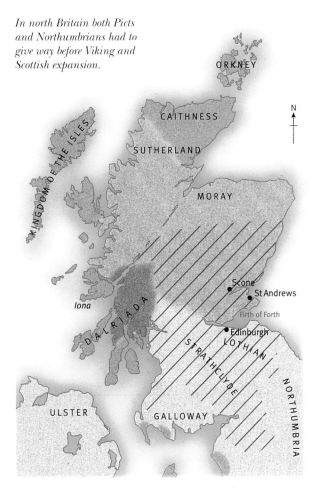

In north Britain both Picts and Northumbrians had to give way before Viking and Scottish expansion.

The Scottish conquests of northern Britain

- Norwegian lands after 800
- Pictish kingdoms before about 800
- Scots of Dalriada before about 800
- the new Scottish kingdom by 1034

0   25   50 km

This is the front of a stone coffin, or sarcophagus, from the church of St Andrews, which was founded by the Pictish king, Angus Mac Fergus. It is thought to be the coffin of King Constantine II, the only early Scottish king who was not buried at Iona. The figures probably represent David as a shepherd and as a hunter.

A new Scottish kingdom

In the north of Britain the ancient Pictish civilization vanished. The Picts were squeezed between the Vikings and the Scots. The Vikings conquered the northern isles, the Hebrides and Caithness. South of Sutherland (the southern land of the Vikings) Scottish kings from Dalriada overran the Pictish kingdoms of the east coast. The most famous of these Scottish kings was Kenneth Mac Alpin, who ruled in about the year 850. Later legends told how he invited the Pictish chiefs to a party, got them drunk and then slaughtered them. It may not have happened quite like this – but it could have done. A king's followers expected him to give parties and to make sure that the alcohol flowed. It would not be surprising if sometimes it was the blood of the defeated that flowed. However it happened, historians know that the Picts 'disappeared'. Their language died out, and their laws were suppressed. Presumably most ordinary Picts made the best of things, learned the Gaelic language and lived alongside and intermarried with the Scots.

From the ninth century onwards the centres of the new Scottish kingdom were to be places in the east such as Scone and St Andrews. Scottish kings were fortunate to have richer farmlands than their rivals in northern Britain, especially in Fife. In the tenth century Kenneth Mac Alpin's successors gradually pushed their way south across the Firth of Forth. They captured Strathclyde from the Britons and Lothian (including Edinburgh) from

the Northumbrians. By the early eleventh century Scottish power stretched to a border which was more or less where it is today.

Immediately north of the Scottish kingdom lay the land of Moray (see the map on page 12). Moray had also been taken from the Picts by Dalriadan Scots. In 1040 the Scottish king, Duncan (1034–1040), decided he wanted it for himself and he led an army into Moray. He was killed by Moray's ruler, Macbeth.

Macbeth (1040–1057) then went over to the attack. He drove Duncan's sons into exile and seized Duncan's throne. He ruled the united Scottish kingdom until 1054, when Earl Siward of Northumbria defeated him in battle at Dunsinnan Hill (near Scone) and put Malcolm Canmore, Duncan's son, as king in his place. This story is the basis of the play by Shakespeare, *Macbeth*.

For some years Macbeth still held out in Moray, but eventually he was hunted down and killed. Rivalry between the rulers of Moray and Scotland continued until eventually the Scottish kings won, and Moray became part of the kingdom of Scotland.

Malcolm Canmore (1058–1093) was to be a great and successful king, but he did not rule anything like the whole of what we now call Scotland. The rulers of Orkney (who also ruled Caithness) and the kings of the Isles all owed allegiance to the king of Norway. In the south-west, Galloway was also independent. Malcolm's own kingdom contained several different peoples, in which three different languages were spoken: Gaelic, Brittonic and English.

Kings in Wales

The people who lived in what we now call Wales called themselves Britons. Although they were united by culture, language and law, politically they were divided into a number of kingdoms. The strongest of these were Gwynedd, Dyfed and Glywysing, but at any one time there were usually several more than these three. The non-stop rivalry between kings meant that kingdoms were constantly changing, in both size and name. Dyfed joined with neighbouring kingdoms to become Deheubarth. One tenth-century king of Glywysing, Morgan Hen 'the Old', became so famous that the region he ruled was re-named 'Morgan's Land' or Morgannwg, which is the origin of the area's name today, Glamorgan. Occasionally very clever kings managed to rule two major kingdoms. Hywel Dda 'the Good' briefly held both Gwynedd and Dyfed. In later centuries all the Welsh would say that they recognized 'the laws of Hywel Dda'. When Hywel died in about 950, Gwynedd and Dyfed again fell under separate rulers.

The Welsh Britons were proud of their descent from the Britons of old. They remembered how, long ago, the Saxons had driven them out of the fertile lands and into the mountains of the west. The growing power of an English kingdom in the tenth-century, with a monarchy that

This sculpted stone cross at Carew in Dyfed stands four metres high and is decorated with an interlacing pattern typical of much early art. A Latin inscription refers to Maredudd son of Edwin, and there was a king of Deheubarth with that name who was killed in battle in 1035.

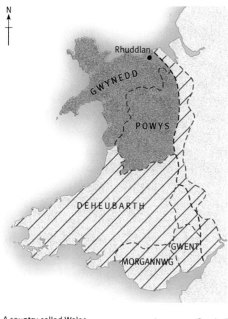

N

A country called Wales

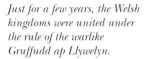

original kingdom of
Gruffudd ap Llywelyn

Welsh kingdoms conquered
by Gruffudd ap Llywelyn by
1063

– – – Offa's Dyke

0   20   40 km

*Just for a few years, the Welsh
kingdoms were united under
the rule of the warlike
Gruffudd ap Llywelyn.*

was powerful enough to demand heavy tributes from many
of the kings in Wales, was an unpleasant reminder to them
of this ancient history. The tenth-century dramatic poem
Armes Prydein ('The Prophecy of Britain') was a call to the
Welsh to join with the Irish and others to drive out the
Saxons; it looked forward to the day when two ideal leaders,
Cynan and Cadwaladr, 'two conquerors of the Saxons …
two lords of profound counsel [deep wisdom] two
generous lords, two noble raiders of a country's cattle'
would rise again and drive the Saxons into the sea.

In the eleventh century a king came to power in Wales
who looked as though he might fulfil this prophecy.
By conquering other rival kings, Gruffudd ap [son of]
Llywelyn forced a kind of unity on Wales and for a while
turned back the English advance. From 1055 he
dominated the whole of Wales. It was the first time any
king had achieved that. He launched attacks on England,
sacking Hereford in 1055 and defeating an English army
in 1056. A Welsh chronicler tells how Gruffudd 'hounded the Pagans
and the Saxons in many battles and he prevailed against them and ravaged
them'. He held court in the north of Wales, at Rhuddlan – which had
belonged to the English. British farmers moved east again, to settle lands
from which their forefathers had been driven. Then in 1062 and 1063
the ruler of England, Harold Godwinson, fought back. Gruffudd was
killed by his own men, and his head sent as a trophy to the English court.

The unity which Gruffudd had forced on Wales did not survive his
death. Rulers returned to their small kingdoms in Gwynedd, Powys,
Deheubarth, Morgannwg and Gwent, so that once again Wales became
a country of rival princes. Most of them owed tribute to the English king.

Kings in Ireland

In Ireland more than a hundred kings of the smallest sort of kingdom
(called a túath) owed tribute, gifts and military service to more powerful
neighbouring kings. They, in their turn, owed allegiance to kings who
were – or wanted to be! – supreme in each of the five Irish provinces:
Munster, Meath, Leinster, Ulster and Connacht. Scores of kings in Ireland
were constantly fighting each other to be the strongest king in a province,
or even to see who could be the greatest king of all Ireland – the 'high-
king' as he was sometimes called.

One of the most famous of these kings was Brian Boru, king of Dál
Cais (in Munster) in succession to his brother Mathgamain, who in
fighting his way to be chief king in Munster had made many enemies
and who in 976 was tricked, captured and put to death. Brian took over
in Dál Cais, and killed his brother's slayer. By 982 he had become the
most powerful king in Munster, and he remained so for more than thirty
years.

In those years Brian Boru attacked and defeated at least twenty other kings. A few were Norse Vikings, like King Ivar of Limerick whom he dragged out of sanctuary and killed. Most were fellow Irishmen. Usually he took hostages from defeated kingdoms, then expected them to join him in his next campaign. In this way Brian built up ever larger armies and fleets. To survive in this ferocious competition for power he had to be very clever and very lucky. One false move, or one illness just at the wrong time, and he could be finished.

Brian knew when to be cautious and when to attack. Attacking a rival kingdom just after its king had died would be good timing. The only rules of succession which anyone followed were that the next ruler would be a man, usually a relative of the dead king. Sometimes the succession went smoothly, as when Brian succeeded his brother. Often, however, there would be a fight. As Irish kings could have more than one wife, there were often plenty of sons by different wives ready to join in the struggle for the throne. Occasionally well-matched rivals agreed to share the kingship. Sometimes parts of the royal family broke away and set up kingdoms of their own. These arguments gave neighbouring, power-hungry kings the chance to dash in and seize land.

By 996 Brian had used these disputes so cleverly that he had become the strongest king in the whole of southern Ireland. In 1000 he captured Dublin from the Norsemen. Then he moved north. In 1005 he appeared at Armagh and had himself proclaimed 'king of Ireland'. At that stage he still had active enemies in the north, especially among the powerful Uí Néill family. By 1011 further victories ensured that his kingship was recognized throughout Ireland.

At this point the wheel of fortune began to turn against Brian. The king of Leinster, some northern kings, Sitric of Dublin and the Norse of the Orkneys and the Isle of Man all combined against him. On 23 April (Good Friday) 1014 at Clontarf, just outside Dublin, Brian and his enemies met in a great battle lasting much of the day. After a desperate struggle, the Leinstermen and the Norsemen turned in flight. Brian's followers were victorious, but Brian himself was killed.

After Brian's death Donnchad and Tadc, two of his sons (by different mothers) quarrelled over the succession. In Munster, neighbouring kingdoms took up arms against Brian Boru's kingdom of Dál Cais. In 1023 Donnchad had his half-brother assassinated. He fought his way back to power in Munster, but that was as far as he could go. Brian's kingship of all Ireland had long since ended. He had not created a united kingdom of Ireland. Nor had he brought the Irish people

The 'Ostmen', as the Viking settlers called themselves, were merchants and fishermen who controlled Ireland's most important ports between the ninth and twelfth centuries.

The Kingdoms of Ireland

– – – boundaries of the five Irish provinces

——— boundaries of the larger kingdoms

▨ Norwegian Viking settlements

▨ Dál Cais, Brian Boru's kingdom

together to fight the Viking outsiders. (Although in later centuries Irishmen came to believe that this is what he had done, and they made Brian a national hero). In earlier centuries a few equally successful Irish kings had claimed, just as Brian did, to be 'high king'. But none had tried to destroy the other kingdoms, and after their death the old pattern of many small kingdoms had returned. After Brian's death in 1014 this happened once more. The map of eleventh-century Ireland remained a complicated patchwork quilt of scores of kingdoms. Like the Welsh, the Irish were united by language, law and culture, not by politics.

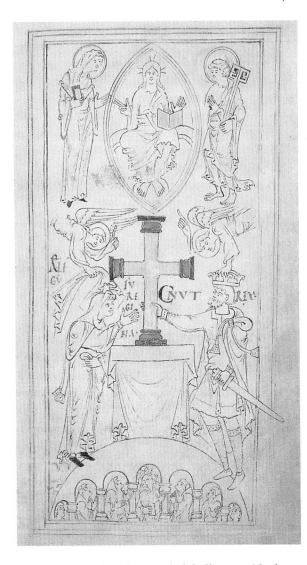

Below a representation of Christ in majesty, two other rulers, King Cnut and Queen Emma (or Aelfgyfu) are shown giving a massive golden altar cross to New Minster, Winchester. Emma had been Aethelred's queen. After he died while fighting Cnut, she married Cnut. In due course two of her sons became kings of England. First Harthacnut, her son by Cnut, then Edward, a son by Aethelred.

Unity in England

England's history at this period was very different. In a crisis the kingdom sometimes fell apart, but such divisions did not last long. In the reign of Edgar's son Aethelred the Unready (979–1016) the Vikings attacked, led by King Swein of Denmark and his son, Cnut. In 1016 Aethelred's son, Edmund Ironside, agreed to share England with Cnut. However soon afterwards Edmund died and Cnut seized both shares. After Cnut's death in 1035 his two sons (by different mothers) disagreed about who should succeed him and that led to another partition.

But by 1037 England was re-united again. Neither of Cnut's sons lived long, and in 1042 another of Aethelred's sons, Edward, known as 'the Confessor', (1042–1066) came to the throne. The author of the *Anglo-Saxon Chronicle* believed that people in England were now proud to call themselves Englishmen. Even when there were quarrels between different parties he wrote,

> there was little that was worth anything apart from Englishmen on either side; and they did not wish the country to be laid open to foreigners as a result of their quarrels.

But across the Channel in Normandy, Duke William was waiting for Edward the Confessor to die.

CHAPTER 2

Norman Conquest to Magna Carta

❖

King Edward the Confessor died in January 1066. Just before he died he named his brother-in-law, Earl Harold, as the next king. Harold was crowned just two days later. But there were three men who had very different ideas about the succession. One was Harold's own brother Tostig. Harold and Tostig had quarrelled bitterly a few months earlier, and Tostig had been banished. The second was King Harold of Norway, known as Hardrada, 'the ruthless'. Soon he and Tostig were planning an invasion. The third was Duke William of Normandy, known as 'the bastard'. William claimed that King Edward had earlier promised the

In this scene from the Bayeux Tapestry, King Edward *is on his deathbed in an upper room of the palace. Below he is shown dead.*

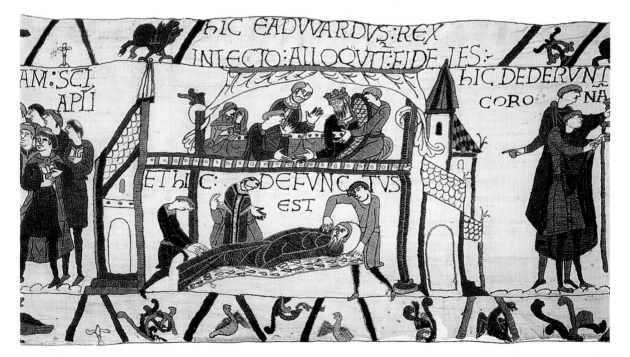

THE BAYEUX TAPESTRY

With his hands on two shrines containing relics Harold makes his promise, watched by Duke William sitting on a throne.

Is Harold free to make his promise to William? This is the important question. Would a Norman notice that one man on the right already has one foot in the water, as though he is keen to leave the moment Harold has sworn the oath? Is this a clue that the designer is following the English version?

The Bayeux Tapestry tells the story of Harold, of how he became king of England and of how he was killed at the Battle of Hastings when Duke William of Normandy invaded England in 1066. But whose version of what happened is being told? The story according to the victorious Normans, or the defeated English?

In the story the Normans told, King Edward wanted William to be his successor and he sent Harold to Normandy to tell William. On the way Harold was shipwrecked and captured by Count Guy of Ponthieu, but rescued by William. Harold then promised William to help him become the next king of England, as Edward had wanted. When Edward died, however, Harold seized the throne for himself. According to the Norman version, Harold had broken his word and deserved to die. William was the rightful king of England.

An English monk from Canterbury called Eadmer

told a different story. He said that Harold asked King Edward if he could travel to Normandy to try to free his brother, who was being held there as a hostage. Although the king agreed, he told Harold that no good would come of it. After Harold's shipwreck and rescue by William, Harold realized that he would have to promise William everything he wanted. So Harold swore the oath, but because he had not been free, his promise did not count. According to Eadmer's version, William was the usurper and Harold was wrongfully killed.

Which of these stories did the artist who designed the Tapestry want us to believe? This is the mystery of the Bayeux Tapestry.

Who designed the Tapestry? It was designed in the eleventh century, probably by an English man who gave his designs to highly skilled needle–women to be embroidered. If he added his name, it was on the last section of the Tapestry, which is now missing.

According to Eadmer, when Harold returned to England, King Edward said to him, 'Did I not tell you what William was like and that your voyage would bring only trouble on our kingdom?'

This scene shows Harold reporting back to King Edward. Does it look as though he is telling Edward that he has successfully carried out his orders?

Who was the Tapestry made for? It is called the Bayeux Tapestry because it has been kept at Bayeux in France probably ever since it was made. In 1066 the bishop of Bayeux was William's half-brother, Odo. The Tapestry often shows Odo taking a leading part in events. If the Tapestry was made for Bishop Odo, which seems likely, it would have to tell the Norman version of the story.

Are the borders only for decoration? Sometimes the artist seems to be using them to comment on what is happening (see below).

Although the Bayeux Tapestry seems to tell the Norman version of events, the one which justifies the conquest, has the artist cleverly also made a design which could be read in more than one way? If he has, has he also left coded messages in pictures as clues to his own alternative, subversive version? The mystery remains.

The spelling of the name of Harold's brother, Gyrth, uses an Anglo-Saxon letter which did not exist in the Latin or French alphabets. Clues like this suggest that the Tapestry was made in a workshop at Canterbury. Would an English artist know and sympathize with Eadmer's version of the story?

So what does it mean when, below a picture of Harold embarking for Normandy, we see a scene from a fable (a story with a moral)? This is the fable of the fox and the crow, in which the crow is tricked into opening its mouth and so loses the cheese. Is the artist hinting that Harold will be tricked into opening his mouth, swearing the oath that would lose him the kingdom?

As the battle approaches its climax we see archers with quivers full of arrows in the lower margin, and then dead men being stripped of their precious coats of mail.

throne to him. He even said that Harold too had sworn an oath, promising to help William, and that Harold, in breaking it, was now a perjuror.

While Harold waited on the south coast for the Normans to attack, Harold Hardrada and Tostig landed in the north. They defeated the northern English army in battle at Fulford, and then settled down in their camp at Stamford Bridge, confident that they had won the North. Suddenly, to their astonishment, they found themselves facing another English army. King Harold, whom they had thought many miles away, was advancing in battle array towards them. They were overwhelmed. Tostig and Harold Hardrada were both killed. King Harold had acted with decisive speed.

Three days later, Harold heard that William had landed at Pevensey in Sussex. He set off south, probably hoping to take William too by surprise. But the Norman scouts were on the alert. The duke ordered his men to advance to the attack. Harold told his soldiers to dismount, stand and fight. The battle lasted most of the day. Three times William had horses killed under him, yet each time he escaped death and rallied his worried soldiers. At last, as evening drew in, Harold was mortally wounded. When the exhausted English discovered that their king was dead they turned and fled. The Battle of Hastings was over.

This is the seal of William I.

The Norman Conquest

On Christmas Day 1066 William I (1066–1087) was crowned king in Westminster Abbey. From the beginning he proved a harsh and determined ruler. The *Anglo-Saxon Chronicle* records how the chief men of the English gave him hostages and swore oaths of loyalty to him, and how William in turn promised,

> that he would rule all this people as well as the best of the kings before him if they would be loyal to him. All the same he laid taxes on people very severely … and built castles far and wide throughout this country, and distressed the wretched people, and always after that it grew worse and worse.

The Conqueror seized the lands of Harold's supporters and gave them to his followers. This alarmed the English, some of whom rebelled, led by resistance heroes such as Hereward the Wake. William continued to make sure of his conquest. He built castles, including the Tower of London, in all the main towns.

In the north of England William punished the rebels by ordering his army to lay waste the

The White Tower is the only part of William I's Tower of London to survive today. This painting, made in the fifteenth century, shows how it once dominated the river bank and the city.

towns and villages. In the 'Harrying of the North' during the winter of 1069–1070 William's soldiers deliberately killed all the farm animals and burned everything they could lay their hands on, including farm tools, food supplies and seed corn. Refugees from the north, exhausted, sick and dying, became a familiar sight on the roads of England and Scotland. William confiscated the property of everyone who resisted him. His followers built castles on their new English estates. Only behind strong walls could they sleep safely.

Domesday Book

Having conquered England, William wanted to know just how much it was worth. In 1086 he ordered a detailed description to be made. In the words of the *Anglo-Saxon Chronicle*, 'so very thoroughly did he have the enquiry carried out that not even one ox or one cow or one pig escaped notice.' All this information was written down in Domesday Book.

Thanks to Domesday Book we know much more about England than about any other part of eleventh-century Europe. It shows, for example, that by 1086, twenty years after the Norman Conquest, there were hardly any rich landowners of English birth left in England. It was a land ruled by Frenchmen, especially by William's favourite Normans. According to the *Anglo-Saxon Chronicle*,

Domesday Book, open at a page on Gloucestershire. The two volumes of Domesday Book are kept in the Public Record Office in London.

the king and the chief lords loved gain – gold and silver – all too much and did not care how they got it. The king handed out land to those who offered

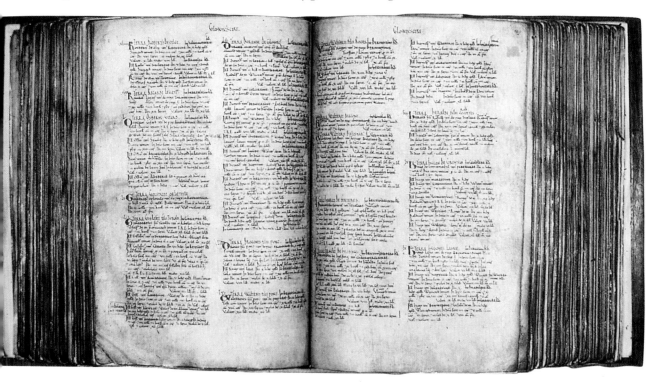

him the highest price, and he did not care how sinfully the money was raised, nor how many unlawful things were done. In fact the greater the talk of justice, the more unjustly they behaved.

In 1087 William died. He asked to be buried in Normandy, in the church of St Stephen at Caen. (He had grown very fat and when they tried to force his body into the stone coffin it burst, filling the church with a horrible smell).

For the next three hundred years every one at the king's court in England spoke French. Of course most of the people of England continued to speak English. Very often the children of the conquerors had English mothers or nurses. By the middle of the twelfth century English had become the mother-tongue of the grandchildren of William's followers. Fashionable people, however, still spoke French, poets wrote French songs and French was the language used in the law courts. Everyone who was ambitious learned French, even though by then they thought of themselves as English. So many people became bi-lingual that the English language itself became (and still is today) a very French English, with thousands of words borrowed from French, for example adventure, beautiful, colour, dozen, envy, fruit, gown, honest. Sometimes they pushed words out of the language. For example, the Old English 'leod' was replaced by 'people'. Old English boys' names like Ethelred or Egbert went out of fashion, and still seem strange to us today, but Richard, Robert and William, the names of the Dukes of Normandy, are very common.

William Rufus and Henry I

After William's death his eldest son, Robert, inherited Normandy. Robert wanted England too, but he was defeated by his younger brother, William Rufus, who became King William II of England (1087–1100). From the chronicles we know that William Rufus was light-hearted, brave and generous – an ideal king, many men said. Most monks disagreed and thought he was an evil tyrant. Why did people disagree so sharply about him? Money was the answer. Nearly all kings were criticized for being greedy. They seized lands or took heavy taxes. William I had done the same, but the Conqueror had also been a religious man, and he gave a great deal of money to the Church. William Rufus did the opposite. He found ways of taxing the Church heavily and spent the

Westminster Hall is the oldest part of the Palace of Westminster, in London. The magnificent wooden roof with its timber vaulting was built in the 1390s in Richard II's reign, but the walls and the overall width and height (78·7 metres long by 22·3 metres wide) go back to the time of William Rufus. At the time it was by far the grandest hall in western Europe.

Kings who ruled both England and Normandy were constantly crossing the channel, together with their friends, servants or soldiers. Government depended upon a system of cross-channel ferries, with horses being transferred very like cars today. In this scene from a contemporary chronicle written by John of Worcester, we see Henry I's ship caught in a storm. On this occasion Henry reached port safely; in 1120 his son did not, probably because his sailors were drunk.

Matilda feasting at her wedding to the German Emperor, Henry V, whom she married in 1114. After he died she married Count Geoffrey. But she was a proud lady and still liked people to call her 'Empress'.

money on other people and projects, such as new buildings.

In August in the year 1100 William Rufus was killed by an arrow while he was in the New Forest. Was it an accident? Or was he murdered? No one knows. His younger brother Henry (1100–1135) moved like lightning and seized the crown before Duke Robert of Normandy (who had gone on crusade, see page 25) had a chance to make a claim. When Robert returned home he and Henry quarrelled.

In 1106 Henry captured his brother and conquered Normandy. He planned that his son, William, should succeed him in both England and Normandy. So he kept Robert in prison for twenty-eight years, until he died in Cardiff in 1134. Before then all Henry's hopes for his son were dashed. In 1120 William was drowned in the wreck of the *White Ship*.

Henry's only other legitimate child was a daughter, Matilda, whom he wanted to be queen after his death. He made all the nobles promise that she would inherit the throne, but when rulers had to do so much fighting, was it safe to let a daughter rule a kingdom? Most men did not think so. When Henry I died in 1135 they broke their promise and quickly arranged for a man, Henry's nephew Stephen (1135–1154) to be crowned king instead.

Civil war

Matilda and her husband, Count Geoffrey Plantagenet of Anjou, decided to fight for her right to succeed. The result was another war of succession. This civil war was to drag on for nearly twenty years. According to the *Anglo-Saxon Chronicle* the barons,

> filled the country full of castles and oppressed the wretched people ... they levied taxes on the villages and called it protection money. When the wretched people had no more money, they robbed and burned so that you could easily go a whole day's journey and not find a village with anyone living in it. The land was ruined ... and it was openly said that Christ and his saints were asleep.

When villagers and tenant farmers suffered, their landlords found rents hard to collect. Most barons eventually tired of the war and forced the rivals to reach a compromise. Stephen could keep the throne, but when he died his own son would not be allowed to succeed. The next king would be Matilda's eldest son, Henry Plantagenet.

The Plantagenet kings

Henry II (1154–1189) was crowned king in 1154. He not only ruled England, he controlled more of France than the king of France. In addition to Normandy he held Anjou (which he had inherited from his father) and Aquitaine (because he had married Eleanor, the heiress of Aquitaine and previously married to the king of France). Henry now ruled over more land than any previous king of England. He wanted more. He conquered Brittany and gave it to his third son, Geoffrey, and in 1171 he invaded Ireland and gave his youngest son John the title 'lord of Ireland'.

In 1173 a tremendous family quarrel broke out. On one side was Henry II, on the other his wife, Queen Eleanor, and their three elder sons Henry, Richard and Geoffrey. Although the king of France (Eleanor's divorced husband) and the king of Scotland joined Eleanor's side, Henry defeated them all. When Henry's rebel sons submitted, he forgave them – no one was very shocked by power struggles between fathers and sons which were quite common. However, men thought it was dreadful for a wife to rebel against her husband. Henry kept Eleanor in prison where she stayed until he died.

Henry's eldest son, also called Henry, died before his father so in 1189 his second son, Richard, succeeded to the throne as Richard I (1189–1199). Like all royal children from the twelfth century onwards, he had been given a good education. He loved music, composed songs in two languages, French and Provençal, and he spoke Latin well enough to be able to crack jokes in it.

He took control of almost all his father's dominions, leaving his only surviving brother, John, with 'only' Ireland.

Like all the other kings of Christian Europe, Richard I had been dismayed by the news that Jerusalem had been captured by the great Muslim leader, Saladin. Everyone agreed that the Holy Land must be 'saved', so Richard organized a fleet and an army and, in 1190, took them to the Eastern Mediterranean on a crusade to free the Holy Land. There he conquered Cyprus, defeated Saladin and recovered the coast

King Philip of France also went on crusade, but he went home early, leaving Richard I to lead the fight against Saladin.

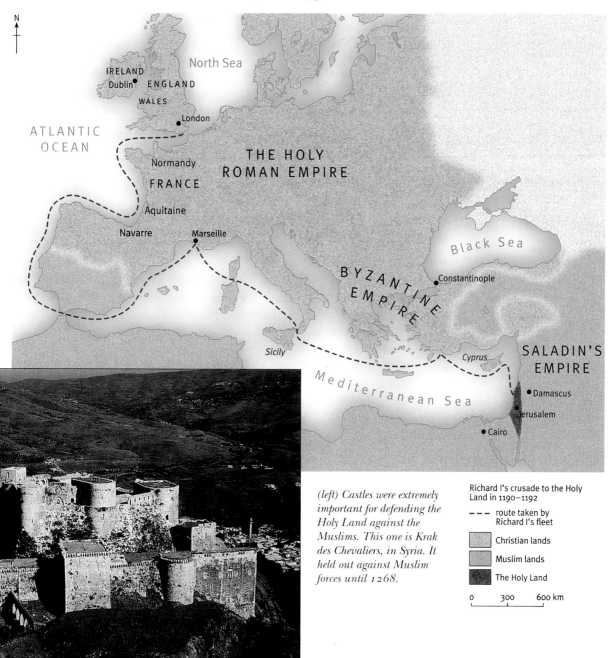

(left) Castles were extremely important for defending the Holy Land against the Muslims. This one is Krak des Chevaliers, in Syria. It held out against Muslim forces until 1268.

Richard I's crusade to the Holy Land in 1190–1192

- - - route taken by Richard I's fleet

Christian lands

Muslim lands

The Holy Land

0   300   600 km

of the Holy Land. Even though he had to accept that Jerusalem itself was beyond his reach, Richard's crusade against such an opponent and so far from home had been an amazing achievement.

On his way home from the Holy Land Richard was ship-wrecked and later captured by Duke Leopold of Austria, a man whom he had offended. For fourteen months Richard was kept in prison in Germany. He was only released after an immense ransom had been paid. While Richard was in prison his treacherous brother, John, allied with King Philip of France and tried to seize the throne. John failed but in France Philip captured some important border castles. So when Richard was freed in 1194, as king his first duty was to recover his lost castles. He had nearly succeeded when he was fatally wounded by a crossbow bolt while besieging the castle of Chalus in Aquitaine.

In his ten-year reign Richard had spent very little time in England. Five hundred years later, historians began to criticize him for neglecting his people, but they forgot that Richard's subjects lived not only in England but also in Anjou, Normandy and Aquitaine. In fact in France and the Holy Land (as well as in England) Richard had taken his responsibilities as ruler very seriously.

Tournaments and chivalry

One of Richard's new plans was to encourage tournaments in England. A tournament was a mock-battle. Two teams of knights fought each other, usually with blunted weapons, on a tournament field covering several square kilometres. The tournament was a team game, but it was also serious training for war, which is why Richard encouraged it. As a successful and famous soldier (soon to be known as 'the Lionheart') he knew that in war skirmishes and battles were won by soldiers who had learned to fight as a team.

Fashionable, rich young men of the twelfth century liked to enjoy themselves by going to tournaments, which were rather like large parties.

In tournaments, just as in war, the knights began by charging at each other with lances. This was called jousting. Then they laid into each other with mace and sword, like woodcutters chopping down oaks (according to one early description of a tournament). This was a dangerous game, for which a good helmet and armour were essential. In this scene we see how a fourteenth-century artist pictured a joust between two expensively armoured knights.

In war a captured knight lost his horse and armour to his captor and might have to pay him a ransom for his freedom. The same thing happened in a tournament, sometimes even payment of the ransom! Tournament champions, like the Englishman William Marshal (see page 96) could win a fortune as well as fame.

'The knights organized an imitation battle and competed together on horseback, while the ladies watched from the city walls and aroused them to a passionate enthusiasm by their flirtatious behaviour.' In these words Geoffrey of Monmouth described a tournament which he said took place at the court of King Arthur. Geoffrey was the twelfth-century author of the History of the Kings of Britain, *a work of fantasy in which he told the story of King Arthur and Merlin.*

Crowds of ladies and musicians came, and merchants brought goods from all over the world. They were meeting places for all those who thought of themselves as chivalrous. To be chivalrous meant spending time at court, learning courteous manners, dressing and living in an elegant style, spending money freely and generously on the best artists and musicians.

Chivalry was about more than polite manners; it was also a matter of life and death. The chivalrous knight was expected to be a good fighter, brave and loyal, just like the fierce warriors of old. Unlike them, he was also expected to spare the lives of any nobles and knights he captured. The kings of the twelfth and thirteenth centuries learned to act chivalrously. They even spared the lives of those who rebelled against them, although, of course, they punished them in other ways, imprisoning or banishing them, and confiscating their property. In earlier centuries, when kings such as Cnut captured their enemies, they killed them.

King John and Magna Carta

Richard and his wife, Berengaria of Navarre, had no children, so the next king was his brother John (1199–1216). John's claim was disputed by his young nephew, Arthur of Brittany. In 1202 John captured Arthur who disappeared and was never seen again. Everyone believed that John had ordered his murder. So when King Philip of France attacked John's French lands in Anjou and Normandy, few were willing to fight for him. As a result he quickly lost them to the king of France, and from then on he was known as 'Softsword'.

This picture, drawn by the great thirteenth-century historian Matthew Paris, shows the sufferings endured by the poor at the hands of King John's officials.

In this century many historians think that this gives an unfair picture of John, who they say was an efficient king. It is true that Matthew Paris was biased against him, but so were nearly all John's contemporaries. They did not trust him, and were dismayed by a king who led them to defeat in war – but expected them to pay for it with their taxes.

John spent the next ten years taxing his subjects heavily, especially his richer ones, to raise the huge sums he needed to pay for a grand military alliance against France. Unfortunately for John, the allied army was defeated at the battle of Bouvines in 1214. The English people, led by the barons, had had enough of high taxes. They rebelled and the citizens of London opened their gates to the rebels. This forced John to meet their leaders at Runnymede by the river Thames in 1215. There they forced him to make promises which were written in the treaty later known as Magna Carta.

John promised to treat everyone more fairly, and agreed to have a committee of twenty-five barons to whom people could complain if they thought he was failing to keep his promises. In fact, as everyone had suspected, John did not keep his promises. Many barons then chose Louis, the son of Philip of France, to be king of England and in May 1216 a French army held London and Winchester. When John died in 1216 the country was divided by civil war. As a king John had turned out to be a failure. He had lost Normandy and Anjou, and much of England too. Although he had many enemies, he almost never dared face them. A song-writer of the time wrote,

No man may ever trust him
For his heart is soft and cowardly

John's eldest son, Henry, was only nine and therefore a 'minor', so a number of barons formed a council to defeat Louis and to govern until Henry III was old enough to rule for himself. The leader of the 'minority council' was William Marshal, now Earl of Pembroke and a famous old warrior. William beat the French in battle. The council reissued Magna Carta to show that they intended to govern the country better than John had done. From now on Magna Carta became a symbol of good government. For the next hundred years, whenever people thought a king was being tyrannical they reminded him of Magna Carta.

This treaty was written down in Latin in a document known as a charter, and because it was such a long document it became known as 'the big charter', in Latin Magna Carta. *Today this copy of the 1225 reissue of the* Magna Carta *is kept in the British Library.*

Governing the kingdom

The minority council of Henry III (1216–1272) ruled England from 1216 to 1232. These were quite peaceful years and quarrels between rival lords took place in the council rather than on the battlefield. This period of peace shows that by the thirteenth century England had a system of government which could work even without an active king at its head. Each county had a sheriff who was in charge of local affairs. In 1176, Henry II had divided England into six districts called 'circuits' and appointed three judges to each circuit. From then on royal judges regularly travelled around the country hearing cases and fining people. Everywhere they went they enforced the same laws.

The king continued to travel around his lands much as he always had done, but no matter where the king was, Westminster was fast becoming the capital of the kingdom. The central treasurer's office, called the Exchequer, also met at Westminster. In the past the king's subjects had usually obeyed the direct commands of the king. Now they were becoming used to obeying instructions sent in writing. A stream of documents sent out by the central secretariat, called the Chancery, was turning into a mighty flood. In the 1220s the Chancery used 3.63lbs of sealing wax a week for sealing these letters. By the 1260s this had gone up to 32.9lbs a week. These chancery records provide much of the evidence for historians about the different ways in which each king ruled.

This picture shows five judges, court officials and prisoners in chains. One prisoner is being tried and others are waiting. The system of circuit judges and their courts meant that everyone had to obey the same law throughout England. It was known as the 'common law' because it was common to all the different regions. The sheriffs summoned juries to attend county courts. This was the beginning of the jury system. Difficult or important cases could be heard at the new central law court in Westminster Hall, London.

Simon de Montfort

Henry III grew up to be a much kinder man than his father John, but as a king he was forgetful and inefficient. Most of his schemes went wrong and gradually the barons became more and more impatient with him. Their leader was Simon de Montfort, Earl of Leicester. Eventually, in 1258, the barons made Henry agree to have an elected baronial council which was to govern in his name. This worked for a while, but Henry resented being treated as though he were a small boy again. In 1264 he went to war against Simon, who beat him at the Battle of Lewes. Simon took charge of both king and kingdom, but his success did not last. The following year he was killed at the Battle of Evesham.

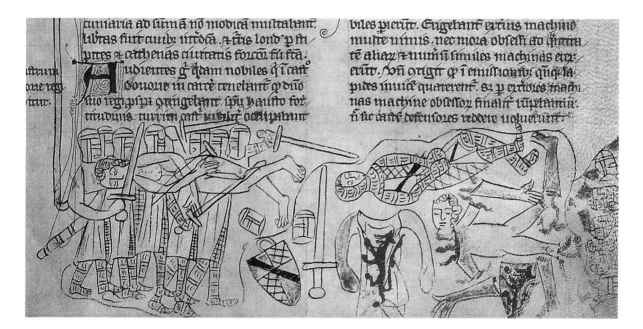

Supporters of Henry III really hated Simon de Montfort. At the Battle of Evesham they not only deliberately killed him, they even hacked his body to pieces. In a period when nobles were usually taken prisoner, this was strangely ferocious behaviour.

It was Henry's eldest son, Edward, the heir to the throne, who won Evesham for him. After the battle he left to go on crusade. He was returning when, in 1272, he heard of his father's death. As he made his way back the new king visited his lands in France. It was two years before Edward I (1272–1307) reached England.

Parliament

In the 1290s Edward I found himself in great difficulties. He was fighting a defensive war to prevent the king of France from conquering Aquitaine. He was also building massive castles in Wales (which he had just conquered, see page 59) and at the same time he was trying to conquer Scotland. War is always expensive, so how was Edward going to pay for three at once? Luckily he could borrow huge sums from the two Italian banking families who did business with kings and nobles, the Riccardi and Frescobaldi. Then he had to find a way of repaying his debts. Somehow he had to persuade his subjects to pay heavier taxes. First he had to meet them, or their representatives, that is men chosen to speak for them.

Sensible kings had always asked the most powerful or chief men in their kingdom, the lords, to meetings where they could talk about the important questions of the day. In French (still the language of government) these meetings were called *parlements*. In Henry III's reign the lords of England still claimed to speak for the English people, so Edward and his advisers were doing something new when they summoned to *parlements* men to represent the towns and shires of England. This is what Edward did when he wanted people not just to discuss matters, but to consent to pay new taxes.

As Members of Parliament these representatives could bring people's complaints and requests to the king's attention. If he wanted to have his taxes paid quickly it was important for the king to listen carefully to what they said. So Parliament suited both sides. The MPs, thought of as representatives of the communities of town and shire, came to be called the Commons. In Parliament they sat separately from the Lords and soon it became impossible to imagine a Parliament without the Commons.

An English kingdom

In the two centuries which followed the Norman Conquest much had changed in England. At first it had been an occupied country, ruled by French-speaking foreign lords. Most of these lords held great estates in France as well as in England, but as time passed some spent more of their time in England. Gradually they came to think of themselves as English, although they spoke French just as well as English. After King John lost Normandy to King Philip of France in 1204 very few English families still owned land in France. By Henry III's reign 'England for the English' had once again become a popular political cry, just as it had been in the reign of Edward the Confessor. However, by the thirteenth century it was quite clear that England was no longer enough – the English wanted to control the rest of the British Isles as well.

CHAPTER 3

A new Church and society

❖

The tithe was the tenth part of every farmer's grain and animals. Although many farmers, like the ones in this picture, objected, all had to pay their tithes to the Church. Rich churches built tithe barns to store the grain collected.

Soon after the Norman Conquest in 1066 the first Jews arrived in England from France and settled in towns as far north as Newcastle on Tyne and as far west as Bristol. Apart from these Jews, everyone else in the British Isles was a Christian. As babies they were baptised in church, throughout their lives most of them went to church on Sundays and great feast days such as Christmas and Easter, they paid tithes to the church, and nearly all were buried in churchyards.

Even today the evidence of thousands of churches, from small parish churches to great cathedrals, built and rebuilt in the Middle Ages, seems to tell us that this was an 'Age of Faith', that Britain and Ireland were Christian countries. Everyone was supposed to be taught the Christian Creed, beginning with the words 'I believe'. Why else should they have built so many churches?

Reforming the world

In the eleventh and twelfth centuries monks, nuns and priests used their imagination and skill to glorify God. They created a huge number of beautiful buildings and works of art, such as cathedrals, abbeys, churches, paintings, carvings and illuminated manuscripts. They had a vision of how the world might be a better place, and tried to make it so. Throughout Europe they inspired the building of thousands of schools

and hospitals, as well as new churches. But these centuries were also a time when people argued fiercely about questions of belief, and in the eyes of many people the monks and priests who wanted reform were trouble makers.

This illustration of a nun is from the Luttrell Psalter, a medieval book of psalms.

To the reformers the soul was more important than the body. Priests looked after people's souls, but kings only ruled people's bodies. Therefore, said the reformers, the humblest priest was more important than even the most powerful king. One of the churchmen who worked hardest for this idea was Pope Gregory VII, who was Pope from 1073 until 1085. Historians call the reformers 'Gregorians', after him.

Kings and lords, not surprisingly, often disagreed with the Gregorians. They found their new ideas disturbing. It was, after all, the rulers, lords of the manor and other laymen and laywomen (those who were not priests, monks or nuns) who gave the land and paid for building the churches. In return, the lord of the manor chose the priest and took a share of the Church tithes and burial fees. Many high-ranking churchmen, such as bishops and abbots, were chosen by kings. In a ceremony called 'lay investiture' the newly appointed churchman received the ring or staff (the symbol of his office) from the king's hands.

The Gregorians objected. They said that churchmen who were appointed by laymen spent too much time pleasing their patrons and not enough time looking after the spiritual needs of the people. They thought it was wrong for the Church to be under the thumb of laymen. Throughout Western Europe the Gregorian war-cry could be heard: 'Free the church!'. The kings and lords did not like what they heard one bit.

In England the problems began in 1095. William Rufus (see page 22) quarrelled with Anselm, his Archbishop of Canterbury – 'his' archbishop because he had chosen him. William called a council meeting to settle the quarrel. Everyone at the meeting was flabbergasted when Anselm said that the question could not be decided in the king's court but only by the Pope, because as an archbishop he would only recognize the authority of the Pope. No one in England had heard this argument before.

Anselm's new argument only made the quarrel worse. Bishops and abbots were rich. Domesday Book shows that they held about a quarter of the entire wealth of England (see page 21). Kings needed men they could trust in such important positions, not ones who gave their first loyalty to the Pope. Rufus became so angry that Anselm decided it would be better for everyone if he left the country.

The next king, William's brother Henry I, invited Anselm back, but he soon got a nasty shock. While Anselm was in exile he had gone to Rome, where he heard the Pope make the revolutionary demand that bishops and abbots should be chosen by other churchmen, not by kings. When Anselm returned to England in 1100, he told the king what the Pope had said. So Henry and Anselm also quarrelled. Finally, in 1107 both sides made an agreement to give up something. Henry gave up his right of investiture, the most hated symbol of the king's power over the Church. In return the Pope allowed Henry to have a say in the choice of bishops and abbots. Neither side was entirely happy. If the compromise was to work, both sides had to agree to meet each other half way.

Murder in the cathedral

When King Henry II came to the throne, he wanted to promote his trusted friend and adviser Thomas Becket. So he persuaded the monks of Canterbury Cathedral to elect Thomas as their archbishop in 1162. But no sooner was he elected than Thomas became a Gregorian, and the spirit of compromise went out of the window. Thomas argued fiercely for churchmen's rights, for example the right for them to be tried in Church courts, not the king's courts. He appealed to Pope Alexander III against the king. Henry felt betrayed. Finally the king became mad with rage and four of his knights rode off to do what they felt sure he wanted. On 29 December 1170 they broke into Canterbury Cathedral and murdered Becket.

Later Henry denied that he had ever intended Becket to be killed, but he admitted that he had spoken angrily about him. In 1174 the king knelt at Becket's tomb in Canterbury Cathedral, confessed his fault, and submitted to his penance of being whipped by the monks. Becket came to be seen as a martyr for the cause of the freedom of the Church. His tomb became the most popular holy place or 'shrine' in England, visited every year by thousands of pilgrims, like those described in Geoffrey Chaucer's *The Canterbury Tales* (see page 36).

This book illustration was painted at Canterbury within a few years of Becket's death. Above we see Becket seated at table when a servant announces the arrival of four knights in armour. Below, the knights, led by Reginald FitsUrse, kill the archbishop. Behind Becket stands his cross-bearer, Edward Grim. On the right, the knights pray for forgiveness at Becket's tomb.

Once Henry II had done penance for his part in the murder of Becket, king and Pope tried to work together again. The Pope continued to have a voice in the affairs of the church in England and also in Wales, Scotland and Ireland. He decided, for example, that Welsh dioceses should come under the authority of the Archbishop of Canterbury but that Scottish and Irish churches should be independent. On the other hand, kings and lords continued to take part in choosing senior churchmen. In this sense the Gregorians had failed, but in other ways the reformers were much more successful.

PILGRIMAGE

What sort of people were the pilgrims who went on journeys to holy places, and why did they go? Some went to pray for the forgiveness of their sins. Others, who suffered from disability or disease (which the doctors had failed to cure) went hoping that a saint would be more successful. They would make offerings at the saint's shrine and pray for a miracle of healing.

The pilgrimage to Canterbury in Kent was the most popular in England. Pilgrims went to pray at the shrine of Thomas Becket, the Archbishop of Canterbury who was murdered by the knights of Henry II. There were many other shrines: pilgrims visited the shrine of Our Lady of Walsingham, in Norfolk, for example, and the shrine of Edward the Confessor in Westminster Abbey, they went to St Patrick's Purgatory in Ireland and they prayed to St Winefrid at Holywell in Wales. Determined pilgrims travelled further, to Santiago de Compostela, in Spain, to Rome and even to Jerusalem, the holiest of places in the Christian world. Sometimes they were away from home for months.

As tourists do when visiting new places, when pilgrims arrived at the shrine they could buy souvenirs. At Canterbury they could buy miniature replicas of the sword that killed Becket, and every pilgrimage place sold badges. The badge on the left shows Becket wearing his archbishop's mitre. The badge on the far left is of the archangel Michael. It may have been bought by a pilgrim to Mont St Michel in France.

An illumination from a thirteenth-century manuscript showing pilgrims praying before the shrine of St Edmund. Edmund was a king of East Anglia who was killed by the Vikings. He was venerated as one of the patron saints of the English monarchy. The abbey in which he was buried came to be called Bury St Edmunds.

This is a portrait of Geoffrey Chaucer, one of England's greatest poets. He was the son of a London wine merchant, and he served as a civil servant and ambassador under Edward III and Richard II. His poems helped to replace French with English as the language of fashionable literature in England. The Canterbury Tales was an immediate popular success.

One of the most famous poems ever written in the English language is *The Canterbury Tales*, by Geoffrey Chaucer. In it Chaucer describes a party of pilgrims who are setting out from Southwark, near London, and travelling to Canterbury.

To judge from *The Canterbury Tales* all sorts of people became pilgrims – the rich, the poor, young and old, men and women, sensible and silly. There was a parish priest who, although poor, was 'rich in holy thought and work'; and a farm worker who

> repined
> At no misfortune, slacked for no content,
> For steadily about his work he went
> To thresh his corn, to dig or to manure
> Or make a ditch; and he would help the poor
> For love of Christ and never take a penny.

By far the keenest of Chaucer's pilgrims was a lady known as the Wife of Bath. She had already been to Jerusalem (three times!), Cologne, Compostela and Rome. She had had five husbands and Chaucer tells us that 'in company she liked to laugh and chat'. For her, pilgrimages were certainly fun.

Some of the other pilgrims were villains, like the red-bearded, bagpipe-playing miller, sixteen stone of muscle and bone, who

> had a store
> Of tavern stories, filthy in the main.
> His was a master-hand at stealing grain.

Yet pilgrimages were not all about sin and disease. According to one preacher, some pilgrims often went 'out of curiosity to see new places and experience new things'. Many were out to enjoy themselves. Before starting their journey, Chaucer's pilgrims stayed the night at The Tabard Inn, in London, where the rooms and stables were of the best quality and they were served the finest food and wine. To make the journey to Canterbury and back more enjoyable, the pilgrims agreed that they would tell each other stories – the Canterbury tales.

Pilgrimages are still popular today, and among people of different faiths. Muslims believe they should go to Mecca. Many Catholics still visit St Patrick's Purgatory in Ireland, Santiago de Compostela in Spain, or Lourdes in France, some hoping for a miracle cure.

This island in Lough Derg in Donegal has been a centre of pilgrimage since the twelfth century.

In summer only pilgrims to St Patrick's Purgatory are allowed on the island.

When the courts began to enforce the laws against priests having wives, many couples suffered punishment. Here we see one couple who have been sentenced to the public humiliation of a period in the stocks.

Priests without wives

The Gregorian reformers said that priests should not get married, as Catholics still say today. At the time this was a highly unpopular new idea. For centuries most priests had had wives and children, and many were themselves sons of priests. There were few schools, so they had learned how to do a priest's work by watching their fathers. Churchmen who did not want families of their own could become monks. Now the reformers, many of whom were monks, said that priests should be more like monks because families distracted them from their 'real' work.

Of course, married churchmen disliked being told that they were living in sin and ought to leave their families. When one reforming archbishop held a meeting of his clergy and told them to give up their wives, he was answered by a hail of stones. But very slowly, with the support of the Pope, the reformers began to win their campaign for clerical celibacy (unmarried clergy). By 1300 it was unusual to find a married priest in England, Wales, Scotland and in the part of Ireland ruled by the English. Only in Irish Ireland were many of the clergy still family men.

The Pope's support for the reformers helped them win their campaign. Gradually churchmen were becoming used to doing what the Pope told them to do. Church law (called Canon Law) said that the Pope was the head of the Church in Christian countries, and more and more churchmen were studying the law.

Monks, nuns and friars

When William of Normandy arrived in England in 1066, there were about fifty monasteries and nunneries, which all followed the Rule of St Benedict. Two hundred years later there were about nine hundred religious houses, and there was a wide variety from which to choose. Although monks and nuns had no property of their own, they lived in communities which did. In a rich monastery they could be 'poor' in name only. Some began to seek a more holy, less comfortable, way to live. They deserted their monasteries either to join groups of hermits or to set up new monasteries.

One of these was an English monk called Stephen Harding. In 1108 he became abbot of a new monastery at Citeaux (in France) where the monks tried to live a more simple life. For example they gave up the linen underwear and black woollen top garment (or 'habit') of the Benedictines (called the Black Monks). The monks of Citeaux, the Cistercians, would wear nothing but an undyed woollen habit, so that they became known as the White Monks. Rich men were impressed by the Cistercians' hard life. They gave them gifts and founded houses of this new kind. The first Cistercian house in England was founded at Waverley in Surrey in 1128, in Wales at Neath (1130), in Scotland at Melrose (1136) and in Ireland at Mellifont (1142).

Unlike the Benedictines, the Cistercians often took in poorer people as well as richer folk. They were allowed to take the vows, wear the habit, and then work for the community as ploughman, shepherd or carpenter. These 'lay brothers' lived in separate buildings and did not join in the central part of a monk's life, which was singing in the choir. Perhaps they did not mind too much. At Rievaulx Abbey in Yorkshire there were five hundred lay brothers, compared with one hundred and forty choir monks.

This aerial view of the ruins of Rievaulx Abbey in Yorkshire gives a good impression of the size of the church and monastery buildings. Only a very rich abbey could afford to build on this scale.

St Francis preaching to the birds. This is a popular image of the saint which reflects his love of nature. To him all life was God's creation. Thousands of people were attracted by Francis's way of life. He despised material values, and he practised what he preached. Many young people decided to join the friars and live a life of poverty. Wealthy parents were often shocked to see their children begging.

As the monasteries became more popular, they received ever more generous gifts. Even the Cistercians found it hard not to live more comfortably. In the early part of the thirteenth century, an Italian, Francis of Assisi, decided to go much further and live a really poor life.

Francis rejected the monastic idea where each monk owned nothing, but the monastery owned much. Instead he started a brotherhood (the Franciscans) which owned nothing. The brothers (friars) were to wander through the world, preaching everywhere they went, begging for their daily food.

Another religious leader of the time, a Spanish priest called Dominic, also took up the idea of real poverty. So the Franciscans and Dominicans became 'mendicants' (beggars). Those who met and listened to them admired their determination to be truly poor and preach the Gospel. All over Europe many thousands of people who shared their ideas flocked to join the friars.

The Dominicans (known as Blackfriars in England) arrived in England in 1221 and headed for Oxford. In 1224 the Franciscans (Greyfriars) arrived. Their earliest friaries were established in London, Oxford and Canterbury. By 1300 there were about 150 friaries in England, about 80 in Ireland, more than 20 in Scotland and 9 in Wales. The friars built their houses in the growing towns. Here their preaching was badly needed, and begging was easier. In practice, even the friars found they could not live in poverty as complete as St Francis had wished. Too many kind people wanted to lend them houses in which they could live for ever.

In 1066 there were about 1000 monks and nuns in England; by 1300 there were about 17,500. In a society in which the population was growing, people were becoming richer and old ideas were being questioned, many men and women were attracted to a life in which they were bound to the monastic vows of chastity, poverty and obedience.

What is most remarkable about this tremendous increase in the number of people taking the vow, is that by 1300 they were all living that way of life by choice. This had not been true in 1066 and before. In the past, many parents had given their children to a monastery as a gift, to become monks and nuns. The gift of a child was usually given with one of property, in order to meet the cost of bringing up the 'oblate' (as that child was known). So many people had had the religious life forced upon them.

Some of the new religious houses specialized in looking after the poor and the sick. In England hundreds of new hospitals, hospices and alms-houses were founded. This is the Great Hospital in Norwich. By 1150 some prosperous southern towns had several of these charitable institutions. Some, like St Bartholomew's in London (founded in 1123), provided care for the poor. Others were for lepers, like that of St Nicholas at Canterbury where, in 1174, Henry II prayed on his way to the cathedral to be whipped (see page 35). In Scotland there were at least fifty by 1300.

Building in stone

The foundation of new charities and religious houses was accompanied by a great surge in church building throughout the British Isles. A twelfth-century author described Gwynedd in Wales as 'shining with white-washed churches like stars in the heavens'. Small churches were replaced by larger ones and new churches were built where none had been before. The people of the growing villages and market towns (see page 47) did not want to trudge miles to church, especially on rainy days. They wanted churches of their own.

Today by far the most prominent survivals of the medieval landscape are the stone churches constructed during the great rebuilding of those centuries. When we think of the Middle Ages we usually think of the Church and the Christian religion. Much of what was written down in those centuries was written by churchmen. But only one or two out of every hundred of the total population belonged to the clergy. How much did other people share the thoughts which the clergy thought important enough to write down?

While we look at surviving churches or manuscripts it is easy to imagine that the Church was the most important thing in people's lives,

This is the tower of St Botolph's church in Boston, Lincolnshire. Even today it dominates the town and surrounding countryside. When it was built six hundred years ago, in the fourteenth century, it would have seemed even more impressive.

Many stone churches were built in Ireland in the twelfth and thirteenth centuries. On the Rock of Cashel, for example Cormac MacCarthy, king of Munster (1127–1134) built Cormac's Chapel according to a design which reflected ideas of reform coming from England and Europe.

that theirs was a world dominated by the Church, an age of faith. Vast sums were spent on building churches, and on decorating them, for example with fine stained glass windows. Yet the rich and powerful spent much larger sums on building and decorating houses and palaces to live in than they did on churches to pray in. But over the centuries since then nearly all medieval houses and palaces have been knocked down and rebuilt, according to ever-changing ideas of domestic comfort. By contrast, people have often added new sections to their old churches, but they have hardly ever demolished them completely. The churches survive for us to see and touch, the houses and palaces – on which they spent more – do not. So it is easier for us to imagine them at prayer than to imagine them at home.

An age of faith?

How can we tell what ninety-eight per cent of the population believed? They were supposed to learn the Creed by heart. They may have done, but did they believe it? One preacher complained that people repeated the Creed 'like magpies', not knowing what they were saying. When one woman said that she did not know whether hell existed or not, a churchman asked her who had taught her to doubt. No one, she replied, she had thought it out for herself. Perhaps, just like today, some people believed and others did not. Those who did helped to pay for the churches, while those who did not found other ways of spending their money. According to a famous thirteenth-century churchman, Thomas Aquinas, those who did not believe were stupid and proud.

In the early thirteenth century King John quarrelled with the Pope. So the Pope ordered the English clergy to shut their churches and hold no more services except baptisms and funerals or 'last rites'. Throughout England the clergy obeyed the Pope. What did most people think when they found the church doors closed against them? None of them wrote down what they thought so we cannot be sure, but there are no recorded complaints, no petitions begging John to end his quarrel with the Pope so that the churches could be reopened.

The clergy, of course, were important in teaching people about right and wrong, but they were not the only teachers. Many popular songs of the day not only stirred the hearts of their listeners, they also taught them how to live their own lives. The songs about Roland and Charlemagne, for example, showed a young man how to behave when in great danger. Through such songs and stories he learnt to know the difference between good actions and those which would bring disgrace, between a sense of honour and a sense of shame. The priests told him that one day he would die and go to either heaven or hell. The songs about the heroes of the past told him that although he must die, his name need not, and it was up to him whether he left behind a good name or an evil reputation. The priests were kinder than the song-writers. The priests said that God was merciful and no matter what a man or woman had done, a deathbed confession and repentance might gain them entrance to heaven.

By 1300 one great change had taken place: in 1290 Edward I expelled the Jews from England. Although some of them were very rich they had never been very comfortable. They had been made to feel outsiders. One English author, a monk of Norwich called Thomas of Monmouth, invented the lie that Jews sacrificed Christian children on their altars. Anti-Jewish feeling sometimes led to rioting and, as at York in 1190, to killing (though never on a twentieth-century scale). The kings did their best to protect them, but the Jews had to pay heavily for this protection. By 1290 they had paid so much in taxes they had very little money left. When King Edward I expelled them most Christians approved.

At the insistence of the Church, Jews had to fast in Lent and wear distinctive badges: two strips of yellow cloth, six inches long and three inches wide. Jews were not allowed to enter churches or to keep Christians as servants. Understandably, Jews tended to live in towns, close to what they hoped was the protection of royal castles. Kings looked upon them as a useful source of money.

CHAPTER 4

Working in country and town

❖

In the centuries after the Romans left Britain, plague, famine and war had killed many people. In King Alfred's time there were probably only about two million people living in the whole of the British Isles. There was plenty of land for all, but not many hands to work it. For kings and lords who wanted power people were very precious, because they were the ones who grew food and made things. When King Alfred wrote down what a king needed, his first thought was that 'he must have men, men who pray, men who fight and men who work'.

By 1300 the men and women who worked had brought about a huge change in Britain and Ireland. Since the 900s there had been four centuries in which the population had increased and trade had grown, especially in England. By 1300 the population of England alone was about six million. England was already, for those days, a rich country. It

This is how Aelfric of Eynsham, an Anglo-Saxon author, described a shepherd's day (although here, this shepherd might have been taking the credit for the dairy-maid's skill):

Early in the morning I drive my sheep to their pasture, and in the heat and the cold I and my dogs guard them against wolves. I lead them back to their folds which I move from time to time. I milk them twice a day, and I make cheese and butter.

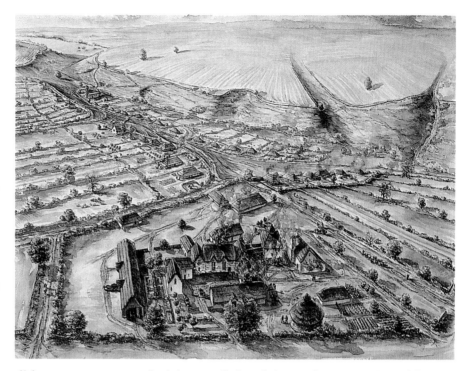

Most farmhouses were single-storey buildings with few windows in walls made of cob (clay and straw) or of timber and wattle and daub. The roof was made of straw, reed or turf and contained a hole so that the smoke from an open hearth fire could escape. The floor was usually the bare subsoil covered with rushes or straw. People and animals often lived under one roof in longhouses divided into two sections.

did not grow very much richer until the eighteenth century. But although the country as a whole was prosperous, the gap between rich and poor was getting wider. Then, in 1348, the Black Death struck. One of its effects was to create a new kind of prosperity.

Farming the land

Between 900 and 1300 most people in Britain and Ireland lived and worked on small farms. They kept livestock such as cattle, sheep, pigs and poultry which gave them meat, milk, eggs, leather and woollen clothing. They kept bees for honey, and horses and oxen for pulling carts and ploughs. Food which they were able to preserve and keep, such as bacon, sausages and cheese, was especially useful. The crops they grew were mainly grain, used for making bread and ale.

Most people kept animals and grew corn, but differences in soil and climate meant that broadly speaking, in Ireland and the highlands, farmers grew oats and barley rather than wheat, and there were more cattle than sheep. In lowland Britain more wheat was grown and farmers kept larger flocks of sheep. Domesday Book shows there were about 650,000 oxen, used for pulling ploughs, in eleventh-century England.

Most farmers were tenant farmers, who paid rent for their houses and plots of land. Whether they lived in a well-built farmhouse with hundreds of hectares or were one of the many in a tied cottage with only a few hectares, they owed rent to their landlords, the praying men and the fighting men who held the great estates. In Anglo-Saxon times most tenants paid their rent either in food, or by working on the landlords'

own farms. At first these landlords did not have enough tenants, so they had to keep their rents low with agreements which both landlord and tenant thought would last for a whole lifetime, or longer.

Slaves and serfs

The most effective way for a lord to control his workforce was to force them to work as slaves. Slavery was the lot of many men and women in Anglo-Saxon England, and it was they who did most of the hardest work. Ploughing, for example, was often done by male slaves. Although there were at least 6000 water mills in Domesday England, a lot of corn still had to be ground by hand, a job for slave women. In 1086 there were still many thousands of slaves in England. Men and women could still be bought and sold in the market place.

The end of slavery in England came as the population grew. With more people wanting to be tenants, prepared to pay higher rents or put in more hours of work on the lord's farm, many landlords found it easy to hire men who would work for low wages.

For centuries churchmen had been preaching that it was wrong to enslave fellow Christians but, like other wealthy landowners, had used slave-labour. Now at last the time had come to take the sermons seriously. Fifty years after the gathering of the information for the Domesday Book, slavery had vanished from the English countryside.

The biggest group living in the country were people called serfs or villeins. They could not be bought or sold like slaves. Even so, people said serfs were 'unfree', or 'servile', because they rented their land and cottages by labouring long hours on the lord's land. Although these 'labour services' bore down heavily upon them, they did not have the freedom to bargain for better conditions.

The making of the English village

In the ninth century most people lived in tiny settlements, hamlets or isolated farms, widely scattered over the countryside. There were very few villages, but three hundred years later many of today's villages had already begun to take shape.

The making of the village is one of the mysteries of English history. No one knows for sure how and why it happened. Scientists tell us that from around the year 900 the weather improved. Summers became warmer and growing seasons longer. People gradually found that they could grow more, and with more food the population increased. Some small hamlets became larger villages, but there may well have been other reasons.

Bigger fields were needed to feed the extra mouths. Waste land and woodland was cleared and ploughed, so perhaps fields around farmsteads and hamlets started to 'bump' into each other. This would cause

Armed with a spear, a hunter goes in for the kill after hunting dogs have tracked several wild boar to their lair. By clearing the woodlands, humans destroyed the boars' natural habitat. Though it continued to be kept in parks, the wild boar was extinct in Britain by the 13th century.

arguments, especially when one farmer's cattle and sheep strayed into someone else's crops. They found they needed to co-operate, and one answer was to have 'common fields'.

A group of farmers would together look after two (and later three) large fields, in which they all had shares of the land. These were held in strips to make ploughing easier. The fields were alternately cultivated and left fallow (that is, to rest), so it was in the farmers' 'common' interest to see that no one's animals strayed into the field which was being cultivated until the harvest was in. They all ploughed, sowed and harvested their shares at the same time.

Working in this way, it was convenient for the farmers to leave their scattered farmsteads and live closer together in some central spot between the two great fields. Where this happened, they had created a village. Each had its common fields, and in the midlands of England this is how most people were to live and work for many hundreds of years, until the eighteenth century.

This map of the land around the village of Laxton in Nottinghamshire, drawn in 1635, shows the medieval pattern of open fields, divided into narrow strips.

The making of the English market town

In the ninth century the few towns in the British Isles were mostly ports, on the rivers or coasts of the south and east, such as Southampton, London, Ipswich and York. These were centres of international trade, places for businessmen supplying the rich and powerful with luxury goods. In his list of goods brought in ships Aelfric of Eynsham mentions, 'rich fabrics and silks, precious jewels and gold, spices, wine, oil, ivory and bronze, sulphur and glass'. This was not a list of things which farmers could afford.

Wool trading; the tax on wool was vital for a king needing money to pay for his wars.

By 1086 there were over a hundred towns in England alone, many of which were inland market towns. The people who lived in these new towns were bakers, butchers, fishmongers, brewers, cooks, weavers, tailors and robe-makers, washerwomen, shoemakers, building workers and carpenters, smiths and metal workers. By 1086 the proportion of the population which lived in towns, although still under ten per cent, was already as high as it would be in 1586, five hundred years later.

As the population continued to grow, so small settlements became new villages and some villages became towns. Between 1100 and 1300 at least 140 new towns were founded, among them places like Chelmsford, Hull, Leeds, Liverpool and Portsmouth. Ancient towns grew in size. By 1300, about 90,000 – 100,000 people lived in London. They produced so much rubbish and waste that a public street-cleaning service had to be introduced.

Guilds

From Anglo-Saxon times social and charitable clubs, sometimes called guilds, were a typical feature of towns. Membership of guilds was often restricted to people (sometimes women as well as men) who practised a particular craft or trade:

Members of guilds liked to get together to eat, drink and talk business, as well as to look after the families of those who had fallen on hard times. Many were linked to parish churches; Norwich had fifty and London twice that number. Membership was often restricted to the richest citizens, and it was in this club that town business was settled. Its meeting place was often known as the guildhall. This is the guildhall at Lavenham in Suffolk, built in the fifteenth century.

weaving, tanning or shoemaking for example. They often insisted that their members were the only people in the town allowed to exercise that particular skill. The earliest known examples of these craft guilds date from 1130. In the next few centuries, as towns grew in size and number, so too did the craft guilds (also called 'mysteries').

In many towns the festival of Corpus Christi (ten days after Whitsun) was a special day. After a great parade and church service, religious plays produced by the mysteries (and called Mystery Plays) were performed. At York, for example the shipwrights performed *The Building of Noah's Ark* and the Goldsmiths did *The Arrival of the Three Kings.* Guilds spent lavishly to put on a good show and paid members for taking part – at Coventry the man who played Pontius Pilate was paid five shilllings while the man who did the cock crow got fourpence. At Beverley in Yorkshire a weaver named Henry Cowper was fined six shillings and eightpence for forgetting his lines.

In the twelfth century new silver mines were opened up in Germany and many more silver pennies were made at the mints. By 1250 more than 100 million silver pennies were in circulation in England, five times as many as a century earlier. In 1279 and 1280 both quarter and half-pence coins were minted. At this date labourers were paid 9d a week (1 1/2d a day) and for 1/4d (a farthing) you could buy a loaf of bread.

Making and minting money

According to Aelfric, the blacksmith thought he was even more important than the ploughman. 'I make the ploughman's ploughshare, and the tailor's needle and the fisherman's hook'. Iron, like lead and coal, was mined either by digging the top surface (open cast mining) or by working small bell-shaped pits. Smelting the iron ore took huge amounts of charcoal so that mines were often dug in well-wooded areas, especially in the north of England, the Forest of Dean and the Sussex Weald. This is how a poet described the sights and sounds of a blacksmith's forge where the iron was worked,

> The crooked codgers cry out for coal
> And blow their bellows till their brains are bursting.
> Huff ! puff ! says the one, Haff! Paff! says the other
> They spit and they sprawl and they tell many tales,
> They gnaw and they gnash and they groan all together
> And hold themselves hot with their hard hammers.

Townspeople and villagers going to market needed money. Some Anglo-Saxon coins had been minted as long ago as the seventh century, but not until the tenth century did English minters strike coins in really large numbers. In 930 King Aethelstan said that every important town should have a mint. Fifty years later there were more than twenty-five mints in lowland Britain, all of them south and east of a line from York through Chester to Barnstable.

Tenant farmers began to pay their rents, in part at least, in coin. Buying and selling for money began to take the place of the old way of trading by exchanging goods (barter). By the thirteenth century people were using money to buy quite ordinary things.

New technology

During these centuries some important technological advances were made. Clothes were mostly made of woollen cloth, and there were improvements at three stages of cloth manufacture: spinning, weaving and fulling. The growth of busy markets was helped by improvements in the transport system. Better designed and faster carts travelled to and fro on the roads linking villages and towns. To speed traffic on its way, hundreds of new bridges were built over the country's rivers, or old wooden bridges were replaced by stone ones.

New ports such as Boston, King's Lynn, Portsmouth, Liverpool, Newcastle and Hull were founded at river mouths or on the coasts. Quays were built, and cranes constructed to load and unload goods.

In many ways the technological advances helped men and women to become more productive. But no one, until the eighteenth century, found ways of making big improvements to the yield of crops. What was going to happen when all the available land was under the plough? The population of England continued to grow. It became a land choked with people. The rich grew even richer, but life for the poor became harder and harder. Poverty, famine and disease stalked the land.

The earliest known windmills were built in the twelfth century along the south and east coasts of England, that is in those parts of Britain which were less well-provided with water power. In this fourteenth-century drawing the mill is set on a post so that it can be turned with the help of a long tail-pole, in order to keep the sails facing into the wind. A step ladder leads up to the door.

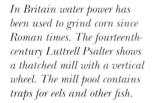

In Britain water power has been used to grind corn since Roman times. The fourteenth-century Luttrell Psalter shows a thatched mill with a vertical wheel. The mill pool contains traps for eels and other fish.

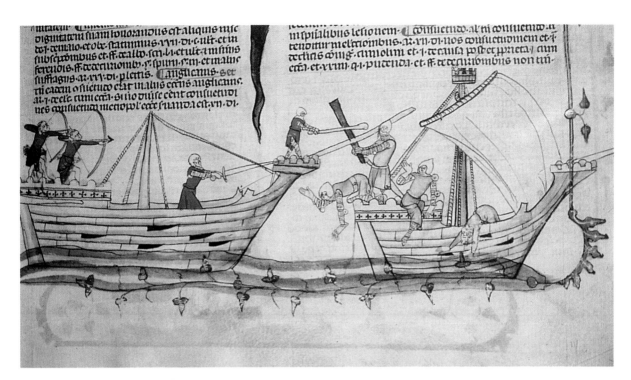

(above) A new design for a bulk-carrying cargo ship called the cog allowed merchants to carry more goods and so increase trade.

(right) Spinning was always thought of as women's work – this is the origin of our word 'spinster' for an unmarried woman. The traditional way of spinning by hand, using distaff or spindle, is very slow-going, although it can produce a fine and strong thread. Even a simple spinning wheel, as shown here in an early fourteenth-century illustration, can speed things up. The woman to the right is carding, loosening the tangled wool to prepare it for spinning.

(left) In the Roman world horses were rarely used for pulling anything heavier than a light chariot. Ploughing and hauling loaded carts was done by oxen. Gradually a number of improvements in types of harness and in vehicle design meant that horses became more and more useful as draught animals. Horse-drawn carts could go at least half as fast again as those pulled by oxen.

At the frontier

The pace of change was slower in some places than others. In the highland areas of Britain and in Ireland everyday life changed far more slowly than it did in England. Coins, for example, were first minted in Ireland in about 1000; in Wales in the late eleventh century and in Scotland not until the twelfth century. People still lived in hamlets and solitary farms. The few towns there were, like those made by Vikings in Ireland, were on the coast. The more fertile parts of Wales, Ireland and Scotland were attractive to people looking for new trade or land to cultivate. Many thousands of English families left England to settle in these more remote places. Occasionally the king encouraged people to move to the frontiers. The *Anglo-Saxon Chronicle* tells us that in 1092 the king captured Carlisle and built a castle there. 'Then he returned south and sent very many farmers thither with their wives and livestock to settle and till the soil'.

The English settlers who moved to parts of Wales quickly built towns such as Chepstow, Monmouth, Cardiff, Brecon and Pembroke (all had been founded by 1135). In Scotland in the twelfth century the Scottish kings invited the English to settle in their new towns. Berwick, Edinburgh and Stirling were among the earliest, with Perth, Aberdeen and Glasgow following soon after.

A large number of colonists from England went to Ireland in 1170 and settled in the older towns, such as the Viking ports of Dublin, Waterford and Limerick. The newcomers built many villages, mills and bridges, as well as new towns in southern and eastern Ireland. For about two hundred years from the late eleventh century onwards, a tidal wave of newcomers flowed into the Celtic lands. Some of the colonists came from Flanders and elsewhere, but most who took part in this great migration were English.

The Black Death

In 1350 a young Irishman wrote in the margin of a book,

> I Hugh, son of Conor MacEagen, have written this in my twentieth year, and this is the second year since the coming of the plague to Ireland. Let whoever reads this offer a prayer of mercy for my soul. This is Christmas night and I place myself under the protection of King of heaven and earth, beseeching he will bring me and my friends safe through this plague.

Hugh may have survived, but many of his friends did not.

The epidemic of bubonic plague, later known as the Black Death, had reached the British Isles. The plague was carried to Europe from Asia in 1347. In 1348 it reached England and Ireland; in 1349 Scotland and Wales. In Kilkenny in Ireland John Clyn noted that in the affected houses almost everyone in the household died. He wrote,

> While waiting among the dead for the coming of death, I have recorded

Bubonic plague was a disease carried by rat fleas. It infected humans when the numbers of rats were so reduced by the disease that the fleas had to feed on human bodies. There was no known cure. Not until 1894 did a medical scientist discover the cause of the plague. Before then three quarters of those who caught the disease died within a week of being infected.

these events in writing. I leave the parchment just in case any human survivor should remain who might wish to continue the work which I have begun.

Some, of course, did survive, but John Clyn and millions of others died. No one counted the numbers accurately, but the Black Death probably killed as many as twenty million people in Europe alone, possibly as much as one third of the entire population. It was by far the worst epidemic so far recorded in European history.

Further serious outbreaks of bubonic plague followed between 1361 and 1362, in 1369 and occasionally later. Although these last epidemics

An aerial photograph of an apparently empty stretch of Norfolk countryside – but crop-marks reveal where the abandoned village of Grenstein once stood.

were never as bad as the Great Pestilence of 1348–1349, they meant that the population continued to decline. Some villages became completely empty, 'ghost villages', the traces of which remain in the countryside today.

Some famines in the early fourteenth century had already halted the growth in population, but it was the Black Death that really changed everything. Plague killed so many that suddenly throughout the British Isles there were too few labourers. Those remaining made better bargains and so wages rose.

Dyers soaked the cloth in large vats, stirring constantly with large poles. For a red dye the root of the madder plant, which grows in Britain, could be used. But for the deepest and most expensive reds, a dye known as 'grain' was imported. It was made from the dried bodies of a type of insect found on the Spanish oak tree. Some cloths were called 'scarlets', not because they were scarlet red but because they had been well sheared (eskalata in Spanish) to achieve the finest finish.

High wages and high fashions

In the 1370s a series of good harvests resulted in grain prices coming tumbling down. The poor now found they were much better off. Their wages went further and they could strike even better bargains with their lords. Some of them could even afford to follow court fashion. Instead of wearing loose woollen tunics, men began to wear hose (stockings) and a shorter, close-fitting tunic, often lined, and therefore using double the amount of cloth. This became the standard male costume, known as 'doublet and hose'. Women also gave up their long, shapeless tunics and began to wear tighter fitting clothes. In 1363 Parliament passed laws trying to prevent people from dressing 'above their station', but it was impossible to make everyone obey the new law. The English cloth industry boomed to meet the rising demand for high quality cloth dyed in fashionable colours.

The end of serfdom

The English poet William Langland in *Piers the Ploughman* criticized labourers for demanding too much and not being humble enough,

> The day-labourers, who have no land to live on but their shovels, would not deign [stoop] to eat yesterday's vegetables. Draught-ale was not good enough for them any more, nor bacon, but they must have fresh meat or fish, fried or baked and *chaud* or *plus chaud* [very warm] at that, lest they catch a chill on their stomachs. And so it is nowadays. The labourer is angry unless he gets high wages.

By 1381 many ordinary people living in the prosperous south-east of England were so angry with the king's statutes that they joined the great rebellion of that year (see page 82). They made King Richard II promise to abolish serfdom. Although he broke his promise as soon as he could, he could not stop poor labourers from demanding and getting better wages. Employers continued to compete for workers, so serfdom gradually faded away as many employers welcomed runaway serfs and treated them as free men.

Although in the rest of the British Isles there was never a rebellion such as the 1381 revolt in England, the effects of plague and population decline were felt everywhere. In Wales landlords became poorer and serfdom vanished. In Ireland too serfs (here called 'betaghs') disappeared from the countryside. Many labourers and craftworkers left Ireland because they could earn more in England.

To keep the cost of wages down, many landowners turned to grazing sheep and cattle instead of growing grain. People were asking for fresh and tender meat, so landowners began to kill their livestock young for the market. Even so, many large landowners found farming for the market so unprofitable that they leased out many of their properties to tenants, who ran them as family farms.

Women and children could now easily find paid jobs, whereas before the Black Death there had been more than enough men competing for the jobs on offer. The increasing money value of women's work allowed some women to become more independent.

Everywhere people were better off and shops were full. 'In all the shops in Milan, Rome, Venice and Florence put together, there would not be found the magnificence seen in London'. Even in villages, more houses were built with stone foundations for their walls of timber and wattle and daub. Richer people put in glass windows. More homes had their own ovens, and more people baked white bread – the rich man's bread, rather than brown. Workers had paid holidays. More people could afford to travel or to go on pilgrimage.

Wages in England remained high for a hundred years after the defeat of the revolt of 1381. Then, in Tudor England, they began to fall again. They remained low for many centuries.

Ightham Mote, Kent. Originally built in the fourteenth century, this fine manor house still survives today because its later owners improved and extended it. For example, the upper part of the gate tower, shown here, was built in the later fifteenth century by Sir Richard Haut, a cousin of Elizabeth Woodville (see page 90).

CHAPTER 5

Conquest and resistance

❖

For many centuries the Irish, Scots and Welsh have tried to keep their own government and way of life while the English have tried to take it away from them. The troubled story of the English attempts to dominate the rest of the British Isles started long ago. The English first invaded Ireland in the twelfth century. They tried to conquer Scotland in the 1290s under Edward I, and nearly succeeded. The invasion of Wales began even earlier, when England was ruled by the Normans.

England was by far the richest part of the British Isles; when English kings and nobles invaded Wales, Ireland and Scotland their armies were far better equipped than were those of the rulers defending their kingdoms. A fully equipped man in mail armour was wearing about eighteen kilograms of iron. Iron was expensive and the English could afford much better armour than their opponents. This is how one Irish poet put it:

> Unequal they engaged in battle
> The foreigners and the Gael of Tara,
> Fine linen shirts on the race of Conn
> And foreigners in one mass of iron.

Although bows were made of wood, arrow-heads were made of iron. The growth of the English iron industry, particularly in the Forest of Dean, meant that English armies had greater fire-power as well as better armour. English wealth also meant that they could afford to build castles like those at Caerphilly in Wales, or Carrickfergus and Limerick in Ireland.

A practised bowman could shoot ten to twelve arrows a minute. Writers noticed that a company of bowmen seemed 'to fill the sky with arrows'. To keep up this deadly rate of fire for long an army needed to be very well supplied with arrows. Their plentiful supplies meant that English archers could keep on shooting long after their enemies had run out of arrows.

Defeat of the Welsh princes

William the Conqueror's followers saw no reason to stop once they reached the borders of England and in 1067 some of them invaded Wales and advanced rapidly. In the years after Gruffudd ap Llywelyn's death in 1063, the Welsh lacked a leader strong enough to unite them against the invaders. Yet it took more than two hundred years before the Welsh were finally conquered. Why did it take so long?

Wales was a poor country, compared with England. Its mountains and forests, and rain, made invasion difficult, and not very profitable. Most kings of England preferred to leave the conquering to the English lords who lived on the Welsh borders (known as the 'marches'). From 1067 these 'marcher lords' extended their power by invading the lands of the Welsh kings. First they occupied the more fertile parts, the coasts and river valleys, especially in south Wales. They built castles and towns, filling them with English settlers.

Naturally the Welsh fought back, and it was during these early battles that the English first heard the stories of the legendary British ruler, King Arthur. The Welsh kings had fought each other for centuries but now, with a common cause, some of the cleverest Welsh rulers were able to unite the Welsh people. When Henry II invaded he was met with fierce Welsh resistance, led first by Owain of Gwynedd (1137–1170) and

In the battle scene above, drawn in the early eleventh century, only the king wears a coat of mail. In the scene below, drawn in the twelfth century, all the knights are wearing mail armour. Between the two dates there was a big increase in the manufacture of arms and armour in England, but not in Ireland, Scotland or Wales.

Llywelyn's son Gruffudd falling to his death while trying to escape from the Tower of London in 1244.

then by Rhys ap (son of) Gruffudd (1155–1197), ruler of Deheubarth. Both became heroes to their countrymen after they died. This is how the Welsh *Chronicle of the Princes* described their defence of their homeland in 1165, and the price they had to pay for humbling the king of England (in the twelfth century 'Briton' was the usual Welsh word for the people we now call 'Welsh'):

> King Henry gathered a mighty host ... planning to carry off or destroy all the Britons. And against him came Owain Gwynedd and his brother and all the host of Gwynedd, and the lord Rhys ap Gruffudd and all Deheubarth and many others ... a few picked Welshmen who knew not how to admit defeat, manfully fought against him, and many of the bravest fell on both sides. Then ... [the king's] provisions failed and he withdrew to the plains of England. And filled with rage he blinded his hostages, two sons of Owain Gwynedd and a son of the Lord Rhys and others.

In 1165 the Welsh won, but against such huge and well-equipped armies they could not hold out for ever. To survive, Welsh leaders realized they had to recognize the overlordship of the English king. They began to see themselves as princes rather than as kings.

For twenty-five years the prince of Gwynedd, Llywelyn ap Iorwerth (1195–1240), was the most powerful Welsh ruler. Soon after his death men were calling him Llywelyn the Great. His son, Gruffudd, died while a prisoner of the English and Gruffudd's son, Llywelyn ap Gruffudd (1246–1282), also known as Llywelyn the Last, followed in his

The end of the Welsh princes

lands of the Welsh princes conquered by the Marcher Lords

Principality of Gwynedd

lands brought under Llywelyn the Great's rule

castles built by Edward I

0   30   60 km

Edward I's castles, holding Gwynedd in a vice, ended the independent power built up by Llywelyn the Great.

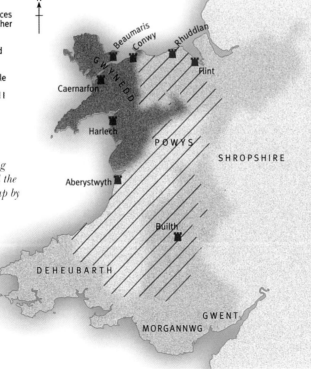

(above) In 1301 Edward I made his seventeen-year-old son Edward, Prince of Wales. The ceremony was intended to set a seal on the English conquest. Ever since then it has been the custom for the eldest son of the English monarch to be created Prince of Wales.

grandfather's footsteps. In 1267 he even made the king of England recognize him not just as a Welsh prince, but as Prince of Wales. In the past there had been a number of competing Welsh kings; now there was a single Welsh ruler.

The new English king, Edward I, hated the independence of Prince Llywelyn. In 1276 he condemned him as a rebel. The following year he invaded Wales and forced Llywelyn to submit, but English rule was harsh and in 1282 Llywelyn led a desperate national war for freedom. In December 1282 he was killed near Builth by a soldier from Shropshire who had no idea who he was; his head was severed from his body and sent to London to be jeered at by the crowd and show Edward that success was his. One of the English commanders, Roger Lestrange, wrote to Edward 'that Llywelyn ap Gruffudd is dead, his army broken, and all the flower of his men killed'.

Llywelyn's brother, Dafydd, took over as leader but was captured in 1283, taken to England, convicted of treason and hanged, drawn and quartered. The principality was seized by Edward I.

For the Welsh these events of 1282–1283 were as terrible as the years after the Norman Conquest had been for the English. 'Is it the end of the world?' asked a Welsh poet of the time. Edward sent English settlers to live in Wales and ordered that English law should be obeyed. Thousands of quarrymen, masons, carpenters, diggers and carters were brought from all over England to Wales. Huge castles with English garrisons were raised at Flint, Rhuddlan, Aberystwyth, Harlech, Conwy, Caernarfon and Beaumaris. From that day to this, Wales has been governed from Westminster.

Caerphilly Castle, begun in 1271 and built by Gilbert de Clare, Earl of Gloucester and Lord of Glamorgan, to counter the threat from Llywelyn the Last. It is only nine miles north of Cardiff.

This magnificent cross (now in the National Museum of Ireland) was made for Turlough O'Connor, one of the high-kings of the early twelfth century, who died in 1156. Turlough had been given what he believed to be a piece of the True Cross of Christ by the Pope and he asked an artist in metalwork to make this cross as a reliquary. The relic was kept where it could be displayed, behind the rock crystal at the centre of the cross.

(below) By building castles the English newcomers drove the Irish back into the poorer parts of the country.

The English invasion of Ireland

Irish lands which Henry II gave to his followers

English castles

0   50   100 km

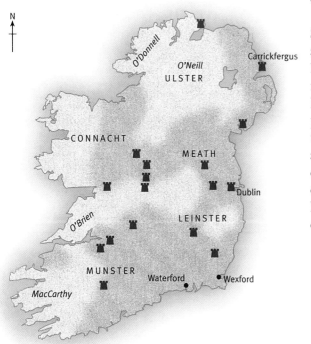

The English invasion of Ireland

In many ways twelfth-century Ireland was just like Ireland after the death of Brian Boru (see page 14). Power shifted between local kings and the king who seized control of Dublin was usually recognized as high-king, a sign of the growing importance of the city in Irish life. Until 1169 the struggles were between the Irish themselves: the McMurroughs of Leinster, the O'Connors of Connacht and the MacLochlainns of the north. To many Irish people 1169 was to be 'the year of destiny', for it was in that year that the English conquest and colonization of Ireland began.

In 1169 a powerful baron, Richard de Clare, nicknamed 'Strongbow', sent an advance guard of soldiers to Ireland to help Dermot MacMurrough, a king of Leinster who had been driven out of Ireland by his greatest rival, Rory O'Connor, king of Connacht. The next year Strongbow himself sailed to Ireland, married Dermot's daughter, Aoife, and then helped his father-in-law to capture Dublin. When Dermot died in 1171 Strongbow took over the kingdom of Leinster.

The English king, Henry II, distrusted Strongbow and decided it was time to act. He assembled an armada of four hundred ships and landed in overwhelming force. From the moment of his arrival Henry behaved as though he were the lord of all Ireland. Most of the more powerful Irish kings submitted to him. He kept the most important ports of Dublin, Waterford and Wexford for himself, and handed out Irish estates to his followers. This is how one contemporary English historian, William of Newburgh, described the result of Henry II's expedition:

> It marked the end of freedom for a people who had been free since time immemorial. Unconquered by the Romans, they had now fallen into the power of the king of England.

The great stone castle of Carrickfergus was begun by John de Courcy. He invaded northern Ireland in 1177, conquered much of Ulster and ruled it almost as an independent prince for the next twenty-five years. King John took over the castle in 1210. Its garrison of forty (including ten knights, five crossbowmen and one chaplain) was twice the size of any other castle in Ulster in John's reign.

Carrickfergus was one of the many new towns which the English founded in Ireland. (Part of the harbour, once vital to the town's prosperity, has now been filled in and made into a car-park).

William of Newburgh was only half right. The Irish fought back and it was to be more than four hundred years before the English conquest of the island was completed. At first the speed of the conquest continued. English settlers crossed the Irish Sea and English courtiers became great landowners in Ireland, although some never went there, remaining 'absentee' landlords. Irish kings lost both power and influence. In the south-east of Ireland, where most of the English settled, the Irish were pushed back into uplands and bogs, the poorest parts of the countryside. In other regions they were more successful. In the north-west, for example, the O'Donnells and O'Neills kept the English out and they lived according to their own Irish law, known as 'Brehon law'. Where the English conquered and settled, however, they introduced English law and government. They divided up the land into counties on the English pattern, and appointed Englishmen as sheriffs and judges. Throughout the thirteenth century the invaders generally held the upper hand.

The making of Scotland

The kingdom of Scotland was much bigger than the principality of Wales, and the Highlands were as difficult to invade as the Welsh mountains. In the Lowlands the Scottish kings began to copy many of the English ways of governing.

When King Malcolm Canmore (1058–1093) married an Anglo-Saxon princess called Margaret, their court attracted many English immigrants, often fleeing from the disaster of the Norman Conquest. No less than three of the sons of Margaret and Malcolm became kings of Scotland: Edgar (1097–1107), Alexander I (1107–1124) and David I (1124–1153), and one of their daughters, Matilda, married King Henry I of England.

One of the earliest royal biographies was the story of Margaret which was written by her chaplain. According to him her husband really loved and respected her,

> Although he could not read, he liked to hold and admire the books which she used for prayer and study. If there was one she was especially fond of, he would take it and kiss it.

Margaret attended councils of the Scottish Church so that she could introduce what she thought were more civilized customs – that is, English customs. She also introduced English fashions to the Scottish court and encouraged trading links with England.

Margaret's chaplain praised her holiness, generosity to the poor and orphans, and the care she took over the education of her children. She and Malcolm founded Dunfermline Abbey, where their descendants were buried. Long after her death the Church officially declared that she had been a saint. Her chaplain's biography helped to create this view of her.

Dunfermline Abbey was built by Margaret's son, David I, on the site of the church his mother had built. The new church was built in her honour. The patterns on the columns (known as 'piers') are similar to those of the English cathedral at Durham, showing the English influence on their design.

When Margaret and Malcolm died in 1093, Malcolm's brother, Donald Ban (1093–1097), and others who hated Margaret's English customs, tried to rule the country, but Margaret's son Edgar asked the English king, William Rufus, to help win back the throne. In 1097 an English army invaded Scotland, captured Donald Ban, who was blinded and made to give up the throne. He was the last Scottish king to be buried on the Gaelic holy island of Iona.

Margaret's youngest son, David (1124–1153), had been taken to England and brought up at the French-speaking court of Henry I (where David's sister, Matilda, was queen). Here, William of Malmesbury, an English historian, wrote 'the rust of David's native barbarism was polished away'. When he returned to Scotland as king, David welcomed immigrants from England and France to his court, discouraged some old Scottish practices such as raiding for slaves and, said William of Malmesbury, 'he offered tax reductions to any of his subjects who would learn to live in a civilized manner'. These 'English' policies were resented by some Gaelic nobles, particularly in Moray, but David overcame all opposition and strengthened the Scottish crown.

Later Scottish kings like William 'the Lion' (1165–1214), Alexander II (1214–1249) and Alexander III (1249–1286) followed in David's footsteps. They worked hard to extend their power both northwards (beyond Moray Firth) and westwards into Galloway and the Western Isles where the king of Norway still ruled. He was not going to let the Scottish kings advance without a fight, but in 1263, after a battle fought on the beach of Largs, on the Firth of Clyde, the Norwegians decided to make peace. In the Treaty of Perth in 1266 they sold all their rights over the Kingdom of Man and the Western Isles to the Scottish crown. This was the 'closing down sale' which marked the end of the 'Viking period' of Scottish history.

King David's ambitions also stretched southwards into England. His queen was a daughter of the Earl of Northumbria, and he claimed that this gave him and his descendants the right to lands as far south as the River Tyne. David invaded twice during the English civil war of Stephen's reign (see page 23) and future Scottish kings pressed this claim whenever they had the chance. From 1137 to 1237 a century-

long see-saw struggle was waged between the Scottish and English kings for power over Northumbria. Finally, in 1237, the governments of Henry III and Alexander II made the Treaty of York. From then on the Tweed-Solway line was the agreed border between the two countries.

The English invasion of Scotland

In 1286 King Alexander III was killed when his horse fell over a cliff in the dark. His grand-daughter Margaret, known as 'the Maid of Norway' because her father was the king of Norway, was to inherit the kingdom, but she died while on her voyage to Scotland in 1290. As many as thirteen people came forward with a claim to the throne.

The king of England, Edward I, saw his chance. He told the Scots that he was the overlord of Scotland and would act as president of a court which would decide the succession. Threatened by an English invasion, the Scots felt they had to agree. In 1292 the court decided in favour of John Balliol (1292–1296).

Edward I treated John not as the king of an independent kingdom but as though he were an English baron. Furious, the Scots turned to Edward I's enemy, the king of France. They made a treaty with him which marked the beginning of the 'Auld Alliance', the long-standing friendship which was to continue between France and Scotland. Edward's response was to invade. In 1296 he captured Berwick, then the biggest town in Scotland, and went on to win the Battle of Dunbar. He took King John prisoner, carried off the Scottish crown jewels, and the Stone of Scone, on which Scottish kings had been enthroned. Further resistance seemed hopeless. England was perhaps ten times richer than Scotland. Most, but not all, of the Scottish nobles submitted to the conqueror.

The oak Coronation Chair in Westminster Abbey, London, showing the Stone of Scone underneath it. After he captured the Stone, Edward I had the chair made to hold it to show the claim of the English kings to be overlords of Scotland. Some Scottish students removed it for a few weeks in 1952; it was returned to Scotland in 1996.

The British Isles united?

In the reign of Edward I an English author, Peter Langtoft, wrote,

> Now are the islanders all joined together
> And Scotland re-united to the realms
> Of which King Edward is proclaimed lord.
> Cornwall and Wales are in his power
> And Ireland the great is at his will.
> There is neither king nor prince in all the countries
> Except King Edward who had thus united them.

Yet Langtoft's vision of a united British Isles under the English crown was soon to be blown away.

Edward I, on his throne, presides over a meeting of Parliament attended by royal judges (in the middle, sitting on woolsacks), lords, bishops and abbots. Alexander III of Scotland sits on Edward's right and Llywelyn Prince of Wales on his left. This is how a sixteenth-century artist pictured Edward I's government of Britain.

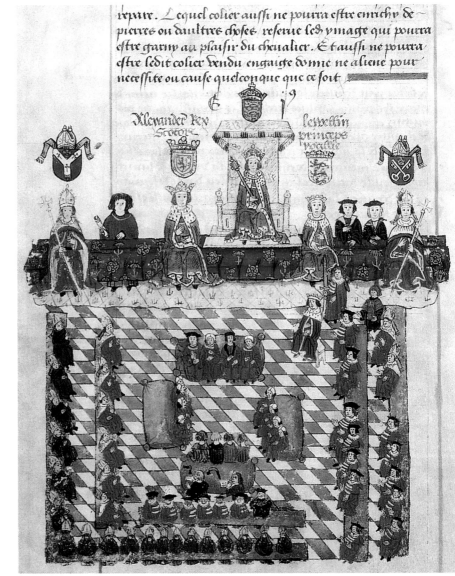

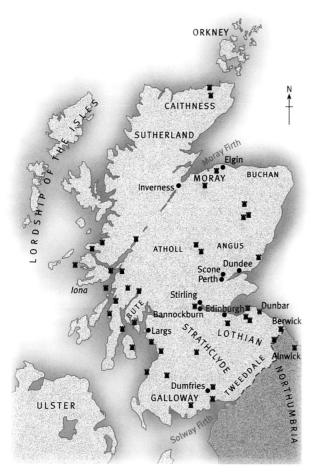

Scotland at the time of the War of
Independence

✠ Stone castles at the time of
Edward I

0   25   50 km

*The Great Seal of Robert I
Bruce (1306–1329), King of
Scots, showing the king seated
on an elaborate throne.*

The War of Scottish Independence

The Scots found a new young leader, not from their royal family but in the second son of a Scottish laird. In 1297, the same year that Edward carried off the Stone of Scone, William Wallace beat the English (who had been sure of winning) in the Battle of Stirling Bridge. Although Edward returned to defeat Wallace, he could not make him surrender. Not until 1305 was he captured, then taken to London where he was hanged, drawn and quartered. By killing Wallace, Edward hoped he had put an end to the resistance which the young Scot had inspired. He could not have been more wrong.

On 12 February 1306 two of the most powerful Scottish nobles met in the Greyfriars' Kirk at Dumfries. They were John Comyn of Badenoch, known as the 'Red Comyn', and Robert Bruce. Robert's grandfather (also called Robert Bruce) had been one of the defeated claimants to the Scottish throne in 1291–1292. Now his grandson had a secret plan to put to the Red Comyn. Comyn could have all the Bruce estates if, in return, he would accept Robert as king. Comyn refused. They quarrelled. Drawing his dagger Bruce attacked Comyn. At the end of the fight Comyn's body lay dead in front of the altar.

Bruce could no longer hide his ambition to be king of Scotland. He roused his followers and rode at speed to Scone, where he was enthroned as king in March 1306. At first few would help a murderer. Soon he was forced to hide while Edward I hunted down and executed his family and friends. But Edward's cruelty turned the Scots into patriots. When Edward said they were traitors and treated them as he had earlier treated Prince David of Wales, it only stiffened their resolve to resist. Early in 1307 Bruce took up the struggle once again.

A few months later, in July 1307, the old English king died while leading yet another invading army. When his weak son, Edward II, became king of England (see page 78), this gave Bruce a breathing-space in which to win his own civil war against the Comyns. By 1314, when Edward II at last launched a great attack on Scotland, Bruce was ready for him. The result was the Battle of Bannockburn, the only time in British history that the Scots defeated an English army commanded by the king himself.

From now on it was Bruce who had the advantage. In 1318 he recaptured Berwick and launched raids against the north of England. Finally, in 1328, an English government at last recognized him as king. Bruce had come a long way since that day in Greyfriars' Kirk. His was a great military and political achievement, but it needed the determination of the Scottish people. In 1320 some of their leaders expresssed their feelings in a letter, known as the Declaration of Arbroath. Although Bruce, it said, was the man who had restored the freedom of the Scottish people, yet,

> if he were ever to agree that we or our kingdom should be made subject to the king or people of England, we will immediately expel him and make another king. For as long as there are a hundred of us alive we will never consent to be subject to the rule of the English. For it is not glory, not riches, nor honour that we fight for, but freedom alone.

This illustration of an Irish harper comes from a manuscript of Gerald's book The Topography of Ireland. *Gerald wrote, 'The Irish are more skilled in playing musical instruments than any other people I have seen.'*

The Irish revival

Robert Bruce did more than beat the English in Scotland. He and his brother Edward tried to persuade the Welsh and Irish to join the Scots in a grand anti-English alliance. In 1315 Edward Bruce took a Scottish army to Ireland. His Irish allies made him 'king of Ireland'. He ruled Ulster for three years and nearly captured Dublin. Then in 1318 Edward Bruce was killed in battle at Faughart. Yet although he had failed to drive the English out of Ireland, he had frightened them badly. They no longer took it for granted that Ireland was theirs.

During the fourteenth century the English began to lose their hold on power in Ireland. After the Black Death (see page 52) no new English settlers came to Ireland and many returned home. Those who stayed

According to Gerald, when a new Irish king was made he would stand in a tub of horsemeat and broth, and share it with his people. Whether anything like this really happened is unknown. Gerald told the story to 'prove' how barbarous the Irish were.

An illustration from a fifteenth-century manuscript showing Thomas Despenser, Earl of Gloucester, facing the king of Leinster, during Richard's second expedition to Ireland in 1399. The French chronicler, Jean Creton says that the Irish king 'was calling himself King of Ireland, where he owns many a wood and little arable land.'

gradually adopted Irish ways and some married into Irish families. This alarmed the English government and in 1366 a parliament at Kilkenny made a set of laws intended to stop the spread of Irish influence. The English were ordered not to intermarry with the Irish, not to speak Irish or dress in Irish fashion, not to listen to Irish musicians and singers. They were not to play 'the games which men call hurlings'. Instead they were to concentrate on archery and other military sports for, said the Statutes of Kilkenny, 'A land which is at war requires everyone should be able to defend himself'.

Although Richard II went to Ireland (see page 86) in the 1390s he was the first English king to do so since 1210. The English retreat continued. By the mid-fifteenth century the English ruled only within the Pale, a heavily fortified line defending a small area around Dublin. Here most of the English continued to believe that they were living in an outpost of civilization, and that beyond the Pale there was a barbarous world.

Throughout these centuries of Irish history a divide remained. There was never a blending of newcomer and native. A Frenchman, writing around the year 1400, described the differences,

In Ireland there are two peoples and two languages. One lives in the good towns, cities, castles and fortresses of the country and in the seaports, and speaks a bastard kind of English. The other is a wild people who speak a strange language and live in the woods and on the mountains, and have many chiefs, of whom even the most powerful go barefoot and without breeches and ride horses without saddles.

Dublin

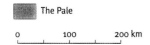
The Pale

0   100   200 km

The rebellion of Owain Glyndŵr

In Wales also there were two peoples and two cultures. An English-speaking minority of settlers dominated the towns and enjoyed the privileges of a ruling élite. The native leaders of the Welsh-speaking majority were excluded from high office in both state and Church. In the end the result was the last great revolt of the Welsh against English rule, the rebellion of Owain Glyndŵr.

When Owain raised his standard against the English in the north at Ruthin in September 1400, the Welsh proclaimed him 'Prince of Wales'. For a few years, while Owain had powerful allies in France and England, it looked as though he might succeed, but on their own the Welsh stood no chance against the might of England. Welshmen who surrendered were generously treated, but Owain himself never surrendered. He is last heard of in the year 1415. As a Welshman of the time wrote, 'Very many say he died; the prophets insist that he did not'.

Edward III and David II became friends during the eleven years which David spent as Edward's prisoner, after his capture while raiding England in 1346. Their friendship did not stop

Edward demanding a big ransom from David before he would release him. Although David married twice he was childless when he died, so that, with him, the Bruce line of kings came to an end.

The Scottish nation

Although the English had recognized Robert Bruce as king of Scotland, the English kings refused to give up their claims to be its overlord. However, once their great war with France had broken out in the 1330s, their chief aim was to conquer France. They made no more serious attempts to conquer Scotland. The struggle between the two crowns became a matter of local fighting between the aristocratic families on both sides of the border, Percies against Douglases.

When David II died in 1371, Robert II (1371–1390), the son of Walter the Steward and of Marjory, daughter of Robert Bruce, became the first Stewart king. He, however, disliked the hard work of kingship and in 1384 handed over the business of keeping law and order to his eldest son, whom the Scottish Parliament said was 'useless'. Even so, when his father died in 1390 he succeeded to the throne as Robert III (1390–1406). At least he was sensible enough to appoint nobles to govern for him, but they quarrelled so fiercely that in 1406 he sent his son and heir, James, to France for safety. On the way he was captured and imprisoned by the English. The following month Robert III died.

The English kept James I captive until 1424,

when at last he returned to Scotland. He announced his intention of reforming the realm. He banned football because he thought games distracted people from archery practice. He executed some nobles and Highland chiefs and confiscated their estates. In 1437 the nobles hatched a plot to kill him. Only when he heard the noise of clanking armour outside his chamber did he realize the danger. He wrenched up the floorboards and hid in a sewer running beneath the house. There, by the light of their torches, the conspirators eventually found and killed their unarmed king.

James II (1437–1460) was only six years old when his father was murdered. When he grew up he found he had a wonderful chance to attack the English because they were fighting each other in the Wars of the Roses (see page 89). In 1460 he besieged Roxburgh Castle. When his wife arrived to encourage the Scottish troops, he ordered his siege guns to fire a salute. One of them exploded near him and he was killed.

At the time, his son, James III (1460–1488), was only eight. In 1469 he married Margaret of Denmark. The marriage treaty gave Scotland possession of Orkney and Shetland. By the 1470s and 1480s Scottish parliaments were accusing him of greed and laziness. His own son led a rebellion against him, and in 1488 he was captured at the Battle of Saucieburn and killed in mysterious circumstances.

Between 1329 and 1488 three Scottish kings had come to the throne as children. Two of them spent long years in English prisons. Three kings died violently. Yet the Scottish monarchy survived all these troubles. Scottish kings never tried to conquer England. Nor, after Edward Bruce's death in 1318, did they try to conquer Ireland. On the whole, once independence had been achieved, the Scottish kings lived in peace with their neighbours. They did not need large armies and therefore did not have to ask the Scottish people to pay heavy taxes.

In Scotland, as in Ireland and Wales, day-to-day life was very different, depending on where you lived. In the words of the fourteenth-century Scottish historian, John of Fordoun,

> The people of the Lowlands speak English; those who live in the Highlands and Outer Isles speak Gaelic. The lowlanders are home-loving, civilized, trustworthy, tolerant and polite, dress decently and are affable and pious. The islanders and highlanders are a wild, untamed people, primitive and proud, given to plunder and the easy life, clever and quick to learn, handsome in appearance but slovenly in dress, consistently hostile towards people of English speech, even if they are people of their own nation. Yet they are loyal to king and kingdom, and if well governed are ready to obey the law.

In Scotland, as Fordoun saw, there were two cultures, but only one kingdom and one nation. The Scots national epic, *The Bruce*, a long historical poem celebrating the heroic deeds of Robert Bruce, composed by John Barbour in the 1370s, was written not in Gaelic but in English. The Scottish kings had achieved in Scotland what the English rulers of Ireland and Wales never did.

CHAPTER 6

Growing up in medieval times

❖

This illustration shows a baby being delivered by Caesarean section, when the mother had to be dead. About twenty per cent of the deaths of married women occurred in childbirth.

Before the medical discoveries of the twentieth century many babies died before their first birthday, and many children before they reached their teens. These sad facts led many historians to believe that long ago parents did not love their children as much as most parents do today. But this was just part of the modern idea that we live in a better world and are better people than our ancestors. There is no evidence for this belief. Although their tools and machines were much simpler than ours, it does not follow that they were more primitive in other ways as well.

'Babies', wrote a thirteenth-century author, 'are messy and troublesome and older children are often naughty, yet by caring for them their parents come to love them so much that they would not exchange them for all the treasures in the world'. It was knowing that children would be a source of joy that helped mothers to face the pains and dangers of labour. Most women gave birth at home, but from the twelfth century onwards there were hospitals for the poor which sometimes had beds specially set aside for women giving birth to a child.

The experts advised mothers to breast-feed their own children, on

70

demand, not according to a fixed timetable. Yet nearly everyone who was rich enough to do so ignored the experts and hired a wetnurse (a woman who had just had her own baby and could feed another). A wetnurse was a symbol of wealth and gave mothers more free time.

Small children would learn, it was believed, by imitating adults. Their first steps and their first words were greeted with delight.

Children playing, with a whip top, a walker and a kite. Most children had toys, such as rattles, rocking-horses, balls, hoops, spinning tops and dolls. They also had their imaginations. A stick became a sword, blocks of wood a castle, breadcrumbs shaped into a boat.

Learning at home and school

A sharp break came when children reached the age of seven or eight. It was time for discipline, time to go to school or to begin training for grown-up life. In the country both boys and girls were expected to help their parents with the farm-work – weeding, stone-picking, drawing and fetching water from the well, helping with the animals, gathering berries, picking fruit.

As they grew older, however, boys and girls began to go separate ways. Brothers and sisters stopped sharing the same bed. Boys joined in their father's work, ploughing, reaping, building, or staying out in the fields with sheep and cattle. Girls stayed with their mothers, cooking, baking, cleaning, spinning and weaving. By the time they were fourteen both boys and girls had been trained for their future roles in life.

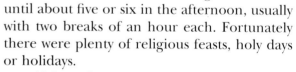

A woman's work was never done. Even when she was feeding hens and chicks she carried with her a distaff, for spinning wool.

In schools for young children, often called a 'song school', the pupils concentrated on reading, although quite a few had already been taught to read by their mothers. They would also learn a little arithmetic and Latin, usually from the Psalter so that from an early age children became familiar with the Latin words of the services of the Christian Church. They would also begin to learn to write, using a stylus to form letters on a wax tablet.

Until they were about seven, children were allowed a great deal of freedom, especially to go out into the fresh air to amuse themselves. Sometimes, like this boy stealing cherries, they got into trouble.

For boys between the ages of eleven and fifteen there were grammar schools where they learned Latin, and the scriptures, a little science and law. The school day started at six or seven in the morning and went on until about five or six in the afternoon, usually with two breaks of an hour each. Fortunately there were plenty of religious feasts, holy days or holidays.

Although a few girls attended 'song schools', hardly any went on to the grammar school. From this stage on school education was only for boys. Girls could continue to be educated at home, with a tutor or local priest. If they were to manage a household, it was useful to be able to read a document and understand accounts.

Very few village children went to any kind of school. Those who did had ambitious parents who could afford to pay school fees, although village priests sometimes acted as local schoolmasters and taught the poor free of charge.

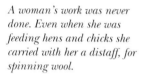

Learning a trade

Just before 1500 a Venetian ambassador to London sent home a description which was mainly about the way rich citizens he had met in London brought up their children,

> Children stay at home till they are seven, or nine at the most, and then they, girls as well as boys, are taken into hard service in other people's houses. They are called apprentices and for another seven or nine years they perform all the most menial [the lowest] duties. Virtually everyone, no matter how rich, sends his children away in this fashion, while he in turn takes other children into his own house. When I asked the reason for this severity, they answered that they did it in order that their children might learn better manners. But I, for my part, believe that they do it because they like their comforts and they are better served by strangers than they would be by their own children. And anyway it saves them money because they don't have to feed these children so well as they would their own!

He obviously disapproved of the system and he exaggerated. Many townspeople taught their own children at home, in the family business or workshop. Girls nearly always stayed at home until they married, although some from poorer families were sent away to become servants, apprentice sewing women or 'seamstresses'. It was more usual for boys to be sent away, perhaps to serve as a page in some other family's home or, from the age of eleven or twelve, to be taken on as an apprentice to learn a craft or a trade. His new master was supposed to be a father to the boy. According to the Venetian ambassador, many an apprentice married his master's widow.

Training for the wealthy

The richer or more aristocratic the family, the more likely it was that boys would be sent away to be educated. In the story of Tristan we hear how a boy was trained to be a knight,

> He learned to ride nimbly with sword and lance, to spur his mount skilfully on either flank, to put it to the gallop with dash, wheel and give it free rein and urge it on with his knees in strict accordance with the knightly art. He often enjoyed fencing, wrestling, running, jumping and throwing the javelin.

At fifteen years old he would become a squire, and by the time he was seventeen or eighteen he was ready to take part in real fighting and be knighted.

The young nobleman would have been trained for more than just fighting. He was also expected to be a fine musician, a graceful dancer, an eloquent and shrewd speaker in several languages and to possess polished manners. This, of course, was the ideal and many fell far short of it, but for several centuries after the Norman Conquest all the English

King John with his pack of hounds. Many kings and nobles were particularly addicted to hunting. They could show off their horsemanship and skill with weapons, as well as their knowledge of the countryside and wildlife. According to King Alfred, the art of hunting came second only to the art of governing – but many kings and nobles thought it was more important than that.

Well brought-up men and women were expected to be good at indoor games such as chess or backgammon. A quiet game for two was an ideal opportunity for the players to get to know each other better.

noble families spoke both French and English, and Welsh nobles often spoke French and English as well as their own language. (Some people of noble birth, both in England and Wales, spoke Latin as well).

The young noble's sister was also being trained in these social graces, as well as in arts such as weaving and embroidery. She was expected to remain chaste and modest, and therefore not to get into the habit of taking too many baths or using too much make-up. She was being prepared for both marriage and widowhood. From her mother she had to learn how to manage, not only her future husband but also the whole household whenever he was away, as nobles involved in government or fighting wars often were. If she were widowed while their children were still young, her responsibilities for family and estates would be huge.

New College at Oxford was founded by the Bishop of Winchester, William of Wykeham, in the late fourteenth century.

In the twelfth century a well-known Italian medical text-book on surgery, by Roger of Salerno, was translated into French and English. Here Roger advises a doctor how to treat a man with an arrow wound. First the patient had to take a bath, then with his razor the doctor enlarged the wound until the arrow head could be safely drawn out. If this was not possible it was better left in. The enlarged wound should be kept open with a dressing to encourage the formation of pus. The dressing had to be changed at least once a day, so it was made with a cord hanging out so that it could be easily removed. Finally, and only when the healing process was well under way, the wound was allowed to close up.

Clerks and scholars

The growth of towns (see page 48) led to an increase in the number of schoolmasters. By 1200 there were so many boys studying until they were fifteen and then wanting to go on to higher education, that a group of teachers at Oxford established the first British university. By 1220 there was a second university, at Cambridge. These were the only two universities in England until the nineteenth century. Nobles sometimes rented whole houses for their sons at Oxford or Cambridge, but most students lived in halls or hostels. Benefactors who wished to encourage boys to study at university founded colleges, many of which can still be seen at Oxford and Cambridge.

At first students came from all over the British Isles to study at Oxford and Cambridge. Then in the fifteenth century three universities were

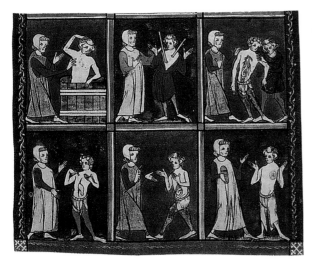

founded in Scotland, at St Andrews, Glasgow and Aberdeen. Plans to found universities in Dublin and, by Owain Glyndŵr, in Wales, came to nothing.

To complete a full university course usually took nine years, so that a student would probably be about twenty-four when he got his Master of Arts (MA), but many just stayed for a year or two, improved their Latin, learned some law and made some friends.

The few who stayed on after getting their MA studied for a doctorate in law or medicine. They expected to be offered very well-paid jobs when they finally left university, probably in their thirties. Some who studied theology (the study of religion) were more interested in thinking out problems than in making money. Religious problems fascinated them. Every now and then they ran the risk of saying something of which the Pope disapproved. One Oxford doctor of theology, John Wyclif, did exactly that. His ideas were condemned by the Pope in 1377 but he refused to give them up. He believed that people should be able to read the Bible in English and he had the first English translation made in 1382.

As formal education was only for boys, the increasing number of schools and universities made the gap between brothers and sisters all the greater. (One young woman did manage to study at university, in Cracow, a town in Poland, in the fifteenth century, but only disguised as a man.) Much more money was spent on the education of boys, on school and university fees or in providing a young knight with horses, armour and weapons. On the other hand, when a daughter from a rich family married she took with her a 'dowry' which would be a part of her father's wealth. Most girls, except for those who entered a nunnery, did marry.

'For better or worse'

In one English village, Halesowen, the records of the lord of the manor show that women usually married between the ages of eighteen and twenty-two. Daughters from richer families usually married earlier, around seventeen, though a few married much younger, even as early as thirteen or fourteen. Girls from the poorest families often had to take jobs as servants until they had saved enough for their own dowry. (This meant that most illegitimate children were born to servant girls; richer people sometimes made charitable gifts to provide dowries for poor girls.)

In Halesowen husbands were usually two to four years older than their wives. Higher up the social scale the gap in age was sometimes much greater. In Halesowen the richer villagers had on average five children, but poorer couples only two.

The giving of a dowry meant that in marriages between rich families wealth, including property, was being passed from the bride's father's family to her new family, where her husband was going to be the head. Often her husband (or her husband's father) promised to give her a dower, wealth that would be hers, if he died before her. Because marriages involved property arrangements, it was only natural that the families should want to arrange them too. Before the twelfth century marriage

One result of the Church becoming involved in the business of marriage was that many marriages now took place at the church door. Some historians believe that splendid porches were then added to parish churches to serve as wedding marquees in stone. This is the fifteenth-century porch of Lavenham church in Suffolk.

was the business of the families involved, and no one else's. Then an important change occured. People gradually came to accept that marriage disputes should be heard in Church courts and decided according to canon law, the law of the Church.

From then on it was the Pope who had the last word on questions such as, 'could you marry your cousin?' or, 'at what age were you allowed to marry?' One important question the Pope had to decide was, 'What made a marriage legal?' In the 1170s Pope Alexander III decided that all that was necessary was that two people of age should freely exchange marriage vows, then they would be married. According to the record of one case,

> John Beke, saddler, was sitting on a bench in the house of William Burton, tanner of York, when he said to Marjory, 'Sit with me'. When she sat down John said to her, 'Marjory, do you wish to be my wife?' And she replied, 'I will if you wish'. Then taking her right hand, John said, 'Marjory, here I take you as my wife, for better or worse, to have and to hold until the end of my life; and of this I give you my faith'. And Marjory replied, 'Here I take you John as my husband, to have and to hold until the end of my life, and of this I give you my faith'.

The court decided that John and Marjory were truly married. It did not matter where they made their promises, they could just as well have been in a garden, in a shop, in a pub or in bed. No witnesses or public ceremony were necessary. They did not need the consent of their parents, guardians or lords. All that counted was that the two partners should exchange vows of their own free will.

Even many churchmen were unhappy about Alexander III's law of marriage. They thought couples should get married in church. But parents and families were especially unhappy. In their view the Pope's law made it all too easy for people in love to get married irresponsibly, sometimes secretly. In practice most children married, and often grew to love, the partners their families chose for them, but some were bold enough to take advantage of the letter of the law, even if it meant taking the risk of being disinherited.

Pope Alexander III's law remained the law in England until 1753, when Parliament decided that all marriages had to be performed by a clergyman and that no one under the age of twenty-one could marry without the consent of their parents or guardians. So young people eloped to places like Gretna Green in Scotland where the old law remained in force.

This picture shows how the Church preferred people to get married – they should exchange marriage vows in the presence of a priest. However, because the Church also said that secret marriages were valid, it was possible to be divorced by claiming that you had been married, secretly, before. In 1483 all the children of Edward IV and Elizabeth Woodville were declared illegitimate on the grounds that Edward had been married already (secretly) when he married Elizabeth.

CHAPTER 7

Gunpowder, treason and war

❖

Before she married Edward II in 1308 Queen Isabella had been a French princess, said to be the most beautiful of her day. She and Edward had four children. In 1325 she visited her brother, the king of France, in Paris. There she met Roger Mortimer.

In 1484 the French chancellor made a speech comparing the peoples of France and England. 'We Frenchmen are good and loyal subjects of our crown,' he said. 'By contrast the English have a nasty habit of killing their kings'. He had a point. Between 1327 and 1485 no less than four kings of England were deposed and murdered. Moreover, it was not only kings whose lives were in danger in these years; many nobles found themselves accused of treason and then executed. Some were beheaded, others hanged, drawn and quartered. Politics in England became more savage than it had been in the previous two hundred years. In the fifteenth century religion, too, became a matter of life and death. For the first time in English history men were burned at the stake as heretics (although it was not until the even more brutal sixteenth century that monarchs began to execute women as well as men).

The end of chivalry

This new cruelty began with King Edward II (1307–1327) who had inherited the throne in 1307. His reign was a disaster. Beaten by the Scots at Bannockburn in 1314, he then managed events at home so badly that civil war broke out in 1321. He defeated the rebels, led by his cousin Thomas, Earl of Lancaster, at the Battle of Boroughbridge in 1322, but then made everything worse by treating them savagely, beheading his cousin Thomas and hanging two dozen nobles. Ten years earlier the nobles had killed his friend Piers Gaveston. Edward was taking his revenge. He felt so bitter that not until 1324 did he allow the rebels' rotting corpses to be cut down. From now on chivalrous practices (in which you treated your captured enemy decently) were at an end in England.

By 1326 Edward had become so unpopular that when his wife, Queen Isabella, and her lover, Roger Mortimer, raised an army against him, there were few who were prepared to help the king. He was captured and imprisoned in Kenilworth Castle. A list of charges against him was drawn up in Parliament and presented to Edward at Kenilworth in January 1327. To make a king give up the throne by force was unheard of. Isabella and her supporters therefore so browbeat and argued with the king, that on his knees and in tears, he admitted that he had governed badly and agreed to abdicate in favour of his son, Edward III (1327–1377). Edward was only fourteen years old, so the real rulers were his mother and her lover. In 1327 they had the ex-king murdered in Berkeley Castle. They

Edward II's chief adviser in the later years of his reign was a corrupt and greedy man called Hugh Despenser. In 1326 the English nobles took a terrible revenge for the hanging of the nobles ordered by Edward in 1322. Despenser was hanged from gallows fifteen metres high, then taken down while still alive to have his intestines cut out and burned before his eyes. Finally he was beheaded, and his head placed on London Bridge.

were nearly as unsuccessful against the Scots as Edward II had been. Robert Bruce forced them to recognize him as king of the Scots (see page 65). This soon made them very unpopular.

As Edward III grew older, Mortimer set spies to watch the king's every move, but one night in October 1330, while Isabella and Mortimer were staying in Nottingham Castle, the king and a small band of friends took their chance. In the words of Geoffrey Baker's chronicle,

> they took the advice of one of their number, Robert Holland, who knew all the secret passages of the castle, as to how they could gain entry by night into the queen's chamber without the castle gate-keepers knowing. Robert led the king by tortuous climbs along a secret tunnel which began quite a way outside the castle and ended in the kitchen of the main tower where the queen's bedroom was. With drawn swords the conspirators rushed in, killing a man who tried to resist. There they found the queen mother almost ready for bed, and Roger. They led him captive into the hall, while the queen cried, 'Fair son, fair son, have pity on gentle Mortimer'.

Edward had him hanged, and sent his mother into retirement.

A ship of war filled with soldiers and protected by bowmen.

The Hundred Years War

In 1330, after the terrible events of the last twenty years, people thoroughly despised the monarchy. But Edward III and his eldest son, the 'Black Prince' turned out to be two of England's most admired leaders, and their success in their wars against France made them extremely popular. These wars went on for so long that historians have called them the Hundred Years War. War broke out when the French attacked Aquitaine again and Edward reacted by declaring that he was the true king of France. His mother, Isabella, had been a daughter of the king of France, all of whose sons were dead, so Edward really did have some claim. In Paris, however, no one agreed with him. There Philip of Valois was recognized as Philip VI. France was bigger and richer than England, so if Edward were ever to be its ruler he would have to fight hard. However he had two advantages.

The first was the fine quality wool from English sheep which was the vital raw material for Europe's growing cloth industry. Edward imposed a heavy customs duty on every sack of wool that went for export, which gave him some of the money to pay for his wars.

Edward's second advantage was French confidence that they would win with ease. Twice this led them to make disastrous mistakes. At the Battle of Crécy in 1346 Edward III's army was much smaller than King Philip's, and the French attack was careless. Their advance was mown down by the arrows of the well-drilled English bowmen. Philip fled, the English won a famous victory and went on to capture Calais, which they were to hold for two hundred years. Ten years later, in 1356, the French again thought they could win easily, and lost the Battle of Poitiers.

The English at war in France acted just like Vikings. Here soldiers are ransacking a house; chests, plate and barrels are being stolen, some break open wine casks, others look for money hidden in pots and jars.

The Battle of Crécy as shown in Jean Froissart's Chronicles. *The French knights and crossbow men, on the left, are beginning to retreat. A group of English archers is prominent in the foreground. Froissart says their arrows filled the air like a snow storm.*

Froissart was a poet and historian whose two favourite subjects were love and war. In his Chronicles *he combined these two themes to produce a brilliant and influential history of his own times. He wrote in French, the language of international culture and politics, but his history was soon translated into many other languages.*

Edward III's military victories made him the most famous king in Europe, and one of the richest, since even in peacetime he collected the wool custom. He spent a fortune on Windsor Castle. Sadly, Edward's son, the Black Prince, died before him, so that when the king died in 1377, an old, tired man after ruling for fifty years, he was succeeded by his nine-year old grandson, Richard II (1377–1399).

The poll tax revolt

Young Richard soon faced problems. The great war against France had started to go badly, but taxes to pay for it stayed high. In 1377 the government introduced a new kind of tax, a poll tax, which was a tax on each person ('poll' meaning 'a head'), making each person pay four pence (a day's wage for a skilled craftsman). In December 1380 Parliament increased it to three times the rate of 1377. Lots of people did not pay. The government sent out officials to discover who had not paid. At Brentwood in Essex, on 30 May 1381, these inquiries led to a violent demonstration and at the nearby village of Fobbing people drove the investigators away. More people joined the protest, first in Essex and Kent, then in other, mostly eastern, counties. Local riots and demonstrations turned into a well-planned rebellion.

On 10 June the rebels in Kent, led by Wat Tyler, captured Canterbury, seized the sheriff of Kent and made a bonfire of all his records. The next day they set out for London. They reached Blackheath in only two days. They assured King Richard that he was in no danger; their purpose in rebelling was to save him and destroy the traitors. This was of little comfort to the boy-king's advisers, who were the ones whom the rebels called 'the traitors'. So they made the king take shelter in the Tower of London. Throughout England the ruling classes, including all contemporary authors, were horrified. Here, for example, is the way the poet John Gower described the attack on London,

> savage hordes approached the city like the waves of the sea and entered it by violence ... At their head a peasant captain urged the madmen on. With cruel eagerness for slaughter, he shouted in the ears of the rabble, 'Burn! Kill!'

On 13 June the rebels crossed London Bridge and attacked the property of 'the traitors'. They destroyed the Savoy Palace belonging to Richard's uncle, John of Gaunt who, fortunately for him, was away in the north. The author of a well-informed contemporary account, the *Anonimalle Chronicle*, tells what happened,

> At this time the king was in a turret of the great Tower of London, and saw the Savoy and the Hospital of Clerkenwell as well as some houses all in flames. He called all the lords into a chamber, and asked their counsel as to what should be done in such a crisis. But none of them could or would give him any.

Later that Thursday the king, sad and anxious, had it proclaimed that the rebels should go home peacefully and he would pardon all their offences. The rebels replied that they would not go until they had captured the traitors in the Tower and obtained charters to free them from serfdom.

On Friday 14 June Richard agreed to meet the rebels at Mile End, hoping that this would give those in the Tower a chance to escape. At Mile End he promised the serfs their freedom and that the traitors would

In this picture two different events are shown; on the left the Mayor of London, William Walworth, is about to strike Wat Tyler, and the king stands by, looking on; on the right the king is shown talking to the rebels.

be dealt with. But while the king was talking to some of the rebels at Mile End (and was in effect a hostage), others entered the Tower, seized and beheaded two chief ministers, the Chancellor (also the Archbishop of Canterbury) and the Treasurer. Then they went on the rampage, killing and plundering. Foreigners living in London were their favourite targets. According to the *Anonimalle Chronicle*, 'so it went on all that day and the following night, with hideous cries and horrible tumult'.

The next day Richard went to Smithfield to meet the rebels again. Wat Tyler, 'on a little horse, approached the king with great confidence, dismounted and took the king by the hand, shaking his hand roughly, saying, "Brother, be of good cheer for in the next fortnight you shall have another 40,000 of the Commons with you, and we shall be good companions". And the king said, "Why will you not go back to your homes?"' Wat's answer was that they would not go until the king had granted them more rights in a charter of freedom.

For a while they discussed this. Then a quarrel started, and the Mayor of London tried to arrest Wat. Wat stabbed the Mayor, who struck back. Then others of the royal party joined in the attack on Wat.

Wounded, Wat 'spurred his horse, crying to the Commons to avenge him, and the horse carried him some four score paces, and then he fell to the ground. And when the Commons saw him fall, they began to bend their bows and to shoot. Therefore the king himself spurred his horse, and rode out to them, commanding them to meet him in Clerkenwell Fields.' The rebels had always insisted on their loyalty to the king and now, confused, they did as they were told. At Clerkenwell, 'like sheep in

This portrait, probably painted in the 1390s, shows a bearded, if still boyish looking King Richard II sitting in state, crowned and holding orb and sceptre. It probably hung in the royal pew in Westminster Abbey to remind his subjects of the king's presence, even when he was not there in person.

a pen' they were surrounded by well-armed men. The Mayor found Tyler in a bed in St Bartholomew's Hospital, had him carried out and beheaded. His followers were ordered to return home.

Although there were more revolts in East Anglia and elsewhere in the second half of the month, the events of 15 June really ended the danger. Once the government recovered, it realized it could defeat the much more poorly armed rebels. Many of the rebels had put their faith in the promises Richard made on 14 June and had begun to go home. On 2 July, when order had been restored, Richard went back on all his promises saying, 'Serfs ye are, and serfs ye shall remain.'

In November 1381 Richard asked Parliament whether he had been right to cancel the charters he had promised the peasants. They answered 'as with one voice that it had been well done'. Nearly two hundred of the rebels were hanged.

A king's revenge

In 1381 Richard showed himself to be brave and clever, but as he grew older he thought that anyone who dared to criticize a king was a traitor, and ought to be punished as one. He also had favourites at court, which infuriated those who were outside the circle, including his uncle the Duke of Gloucester and his cousin Henry Bolingbroke (so-called because he was born at Bolingbroke, in Lincolnshire) as well as some of the other powerful nobles. They plotted the downfall of these 'favourites' and in 1388 the king had to watch helplessly while a hostile Parliament, known as the 'Merciless Parliament', condemned his friends as traitors.

For the next nine years Richard waited to take his revenge. In 1397 he arrested his uncle Gloucester and the Earls of Arundel and Warwick. Not long afterwards, Gloucester was found dead in prison. Arundel and Warwick were tried for treason in Parliament at Westminster. Four thousand of the king's archers surrounded Parliament and, according to Adam of Usk, who was there, whenever there was any commotion in Parliament, 'the archers bent their bows and drew their arrows to the ear, to the great terror of all who were there'.

Arundel, who denied that he was a traitor, was found guilty and beheaded. Warwick pleaded guilty, 'wailing and weeping and whining like a wretched old woman'. He was sentenced to life imprisonment. Parliament then granted Richard the right to collect the wool custom for the rest of his life. Later, in 1398, Richard banished two more of his old opponents: the Earls of Nottingham (Mowbray) and Derby (Bolingbroke). This is the scene with which Shakespeare opens his play *Richard II*.

In 1399 Henry Bolingbroke's father, John of Gaunt, Duke of Lancaster, and by far the richest member of the English aristocracy, died. Richard, who had already taken over the estates of Gloucester, Warwick, Arundel and Mowbray, confiscated the vast Lancaster estates, which by

Northumberland, on his knees before the altar is taking the oath while Richard looks on. According to Jean Creton, who was an eyewitness of the scene, the earl's blood must have run cold as he swore. But the earl was not the only liar in Conwy Castle that day. Creton reports that Richard told his friends that 'whatever promises I might make to the earl, he will be put to a bitter death for this outrage.'

rights should have been inherited by Henry Bolingbroke. Richard was now so rich that he would never have to call Parliament again. He could rule just as he liked. In this confident mood, he left for Ireland in May 1399.

Two months later Bolingbroke returned from exile; he had come, he said, to claim, his inheritance. Henry Percy, Earl of Northumberland, and his son Henry ('Hotspur'), supported him and others followed. Richard returned from Ireland 'in the full glory of war and wealth', but found no one willing to help him. He took refuge in Conwy Castle in north Wales. Northumberland promised Richard that he could keep his throne if he restored Bolingbroke's inheritance. Richard accepted these promises, came out of Conwy and was promptly made prisoner.

Seizing the throne

With Richard in his power, the way was now open for Bolingbroke to seize the crown for the House of Lancaster. Although he had no real right, he claimed to be king and was proclaimed Henry IV (1399–1413) on 30 September 1399. He had taken the throne by trickery and force. Plots by his enemies made Henry decide that he would not feel

Warkworth Castle was one of the most important castles of the Percy family. The rebellion of 1403 was planned within its walls. In 1405 Henry IV besieged it, forcing its surrender after a few shots from his cannon – an early success for gunpowder.

safe until Richard was dead. Early in 1400 Richard was murdered.

In 1403 Henry received a shock when the powerful Percy family rebelled against him, but he held his nerve and defeated them, killing Hotspur, at the Battle of Shrewsbury. After another rebellion involving the Archbishop of York in 1405, he executed the Archbishop. The most dangerous of his enemies was Owain Glyndŵr, leader of the great Welsh revolt which went on for twelve years (see page 68). By sheer determination Henry wore them all down and so, although in the last years of his life he was often seriously ill, he was able to pass the throne on to his eldest son, Henry V (1413–1422) when he died in 1413.

At a critical moment in the Battle of Agincourt the order was given to kill prisoners. Here one of the dead is being stripped of his valuable armour. On the right, two soldiers are haggling over their loot.

Henry V and the invasion of France

As soon as he became king, Henry V prepared to invade France. The time seemed right: the French had no strong ruler because the unfortunate King Charles VI suffered from fits of insanity. On 15 October 1415 Henry and a small English army won a staggering victory over the French at the Battle of Agincourt. Tragically for the French, they made the same blunder that they had made at Crécy and Poitiers. The events of that one day, St Crispin's Day, made Henry a hero.

> No king of England ever achieved so much in so short a time and returned home with so great and glorious a triumph. To God alone be the honour and glory, for ever and ever. Amen.

These words, written by Henry's own chaplain, reflected the king's belief that God was on his side in the war against France. For the next five years enthusiastic Parliaments voted Henry all the money he needed, and never again did a French army dare to stand in his way. In 1417 his guns forced Normandy to surrender.

Henry forced Charles VI to disinherit his son, the Dauphin, and to recognize Henry, (who married Charles's daughter Katherine de Valois in 1420) as his heir. But the soldier king died of dysentery in September 1422. Had he lived a month longer he would have become king of France on his father-in-law's death.

Some historians have wondered whether Henry V's brilliant way of seizing opportunities was not leading to conquests which, in the longer run, he would not be able to hold. But the English held their lands in France and made money out of them for another twenty years. In his short reign Henry V made a great name for himself, not only with the English but also with his enemies.

King of England – and France

Henry and Katherine had only one child, Henry VI (1422–1461; 1470–1471). He was just nine months old when he succeeded his father as king of England in September 1422. The following month, when his mother's father, Charles VI of France, died, he became king of France as well. In December 1431 he was taken to Paris and crowned in the cathedral of Nôtre Dame. There was, however, another king in France. In central and southern France people recognized Charles VI's 'disinherited' son as Charles VII.

Among Charles VII's many supporters was a farmer's daughter, Joan of Arc. When she was only seventeen years old, Joan amazed all who met her by her faith in God, in herself and in Charles VII. In 1429 she persuaded Charles to let her wear armour and ride at the head of his armies. At last his troops began to win some victories against the English, but in 1430 Joan was captured, put on trial, and convicted of heresy. On 30 May 1431 she was burned at the stake in Rouen.

More than twenty years after Joan of Arc's death, between 1455 and 1456, after Charles VII had won Normandy back, a new trial was held in Rouen. This one decided that Joan had been wrongly convicted. Eventually, in 1920, the Roman Catholic Church decided that she had been a saint.

In 1429 she had written an open letter to the English: 'Deliver to the Maid who has been sent by God, the keys of all the good towns you have taken in France ... King of England, if you do not do this, I am battle commander and I shall drive your people from France for to this end I have been sent here by God, King of Heaven.'

Some English commanders hoped that with the 'French witch' dead they would once again be able to push on with the conquest of France. They were to be disappointed. As Henry VI, their king of France, grew up he showed no interest in war. He never even re-visited his French kingdom. The French king, Charles VII, seized his opportunity.

In 1445 Henry had married a French princess, Margaret of Anjou. Partly to please her, he tried to make peace with her uncle, Charles VII, but the English still controlled much of France. Charles had no intention of agreeing to let them keep that. In lightning campaigns in 1449 and 1450 French armies re-conquered Normandy and Aquitaine. The sudden loss of all their territories in France, except for the port of Calais, shocked everyone. Aquitaine, after all, had belonged to the kings of England for the last three hundred years. In 1453 Henry VI suffered a total breakdown.

The 'Wars of the Roses'

According to one observer, Edward IV 'was so genial in his greeting that if ever he saw a new arrival at court bewildered at his appearance and royal magnificence, he would give him courage to speak by laying a kindly hand on his shoulder'.

Although he partly recovered, Henry remained a sad and feeble figure. Born to rule two kingdoms, he would have found the task of being lord of a single manor beyond him. For his subjects his reign was a disaster. Civil war broke out in 1455 and, in the end, thousands died as two hostile parties fought each other for the right to govern.

On one side was the House of Lancaster and the court party led by Henry's wife, Margaret of Anjou; on the other were the friends of Richard, Duke of York, who blamed the court party for the humiliating losses in France. Historians now call the struggle between them 'The Wars of the Roses' – the red rose of Lancaster and the white rose of York – but it was a name given to the wars much later and never used at the time.

These civil wars came to a head between July 1460 and March 1461. First the Earl of Warwick won the Battle of Northampton (July 1460) for York, but the Yorkists governed England for only a few months. The Lancastrians defeated them at the Battles of Wakefield (December 1460) and St Albans (February 1461). The Lancastrian recovery of power was even shorter. The very next month the Yorkists won the bloody Battle of Towton. No other nine-month period of English history saw such violent swings of power from one side to the other as battle followed battle. At the end of it all a new king was on the throne, Edward IV (1461–1470; 1471–1483), the eighteen-year-old son of Richard of York (who had been killed at Wakefield). Margaret, her husband and her seven-year-old son fled the country.

Being a king came easily to Edward. He had the politician's supreme gift of never forgetting a face, and he used it to put people at their ease and flatter them. An Italian businessman in London described Edward's way of persuading people to part with their money,

> I have many times seen our neighbours here when they were summoned before the King. When they went, they looked as though they were going to the gallows. When they returned they were in high spirits, saying they did not regret the money they had paid because they had talked with the King, he had welcomed them as though he had always known them and had spoken so many kind words. ... he plucked the feathers from the magpies without making them cry out.

In 1465 the last of Edward's problems seemed to be solved when the fugitive Henry VI was captured and taken to the Tower. In fact just one year earlier Edward had done something which was to create all sorts of new problems. He had married. His wife was Elizabeth Woodville, an Englishwoman whose father was a country gentleman. Edward had married 'beneath him', for kings were expected to marry foreign princesses. Even worse, Elizabeth came to him as part of a Woodville package; she had many relatives all needing to be provided for. Edward knew he was making a political mistake, so he kept the marriage secret for as long as he could. When the secret was out, observers at court were quick to draw the obvious conclusion. 'Now take heed', wrote one, 'what love may do'.

The end of Lancaster

As the Woodville influence at court grew, so two men became increasingly disgruntled. One was the Earl of Warwick, Edward's chief ally in the crisis of 1461; the other was Edward's younger brother, the Duke of Clarence. In 1470 they forced Edward to flee to Holland. Then they took Henry VI out of the Tower and made him king again.

Queen Margaret agreed to return from exile in France, but she still distrusted Warwick 'the Kingmaker'. While she hesitated, Edward struck. He persuaded Clarence to change sides and then the two of them defeated and killed Warwick at the Battle of Barnet on Easter Sunday, 1471. On that same day Margaret's Lancastrian army landed on the south coast. It was intercepted by Edward IV at Tewkesbury. Margaret's son, Edward Prince of Wales, was killed. The House of Lancaster had been defeated. The first period of Henry's reign had lasted from 1422 until 1461; the second for only six months during Edward's exile, between November 1470 and April 1471.

Soon after Edward's return to London, he let it be known officially

The execution of a Lancastrian, Edmund Beaufort, Duke of Somerset, after the Yorkist victory at Tewkesbury.

This is an illustration from the Arrival in England of Edward IV, *an 'official' Yorkist version of the return of Edward IV and his recovery of the throne from Henry. Edmund Beaufort's father had been one of Henry VI's most loyal supporters. After he was killed by Yorkists in 1455, his sons, Henry and Edmund, wanted revenge. They fought against Edward IV whenever they had the chance. Eventually they both paid for this with their lives. Henry was executed in 1464 and Edmund in 1471.*

that Henry VI had 'died of pure displeasure and melancholy'. The House of Lancaster was at an end. While Edward was in exile his wife had taken sanctuary in Westminster Abbey and there she had given birth to Edward, their first-born son. The future of the House of York seemed assured.

York against York

When Edward IV died on 9 April 1483, he was succeeded by his twelve-year-old son Edward V. On 30 April, on his way to London for the coronation which had been fixed for 4 May, Edward was 'taken' into the 'safe-keeping' of his uncle, Richard Duke of Gloucester. When Elizabeth heard this news, she once again took sanctuary in Westminster Abbey. In June all the children of Edward IV and Elizabeth Woodville were declared illegitimate, and Richard of Gloucester seized the throne as Richard III (1483–1485).

So unpopular were the Woodvilles that many were willing to accept this new king, but soon rumours spread about Richard. People were saying that he had murdered Edward V and his younger brother, 'the Princes in the Tower'. If Richard had killed the princes, then who should the next king be? The candidate with the best claim was an unknown Lancastrian from a Welsh family now living in exile in France, called Henry Tudor. Was it his friends who had spread these rumours? In recent times Richard III has found many defenders. What part he actually took in the 'mystery of the Princes' no one really knows. Two things are certain. One is that the murder of innocent children appalled people just as much then as now. The second is that Richard never made any attempt to prove that the princes were still alive.

Henry Tudor

In August 1485 Henry Tudor landed with an army at Milford Haven and marched to find Richard III. Richard summoned a large army and met Henry at Dadlington, south of the small town of Market Bosworth, in Leicestershire. Most of the four thousand of Henry's troops were soldiers from France and Scotland, England's old enemies. As Henry advanced, most of Richard's army refused to fight. At the last moment some of Richard's commanders even switched sides and fought for Henry. Enraged, Richard charged straight at Henry's household squadron. Even a critic of Richard, like the chronicler John Rous, could only admire the courage with which he went to his death,

> He bore himself like a noble soldier and honourably defended himself to his last breath, shouting again and again that he was betrayed, and crying "Treason! Treason! Treason!"

The new king, Henry VII (1485–1509) put an end to the Wars of the Roses. The wars had lasted for over thirty years, but armies were on the march for only about twelve months in all, and did not usually ravage the countryside as the English armies did in France. So the economic damage was small. But for kings and barons, the leaders of English society, the wars had a devastating impact: more than fifty of them had been killed, murdered or executed. Now they wanted peace, which made Henry VII's task of governing the country a great deal easier.

Richard III's actions in 1483 had shocked so many Yorkists that Henry Tudor had been able to present himself as much as a Yorkist as a Lancastrian. This is why, at Christmas 1483, while still in exile, he had publicly promised to marry a woman he had never seen, Edward IV's eldest daughter, Elizabeth of York. In January 1486 he carried out his promise and, we are told, soon grew to love her.

In 1485, when he became king, Henry had only one real rival for the throne, the ten-year-old Earl of Warwick, son of the Duke of Clarence. Henry kept him in prison until 1499 when he had him executed. With no real claimants to the throne, those who opposed Henry were driven to use 'pretenders' or impostors. First they trained a boy called Lambert Simnel to pretend to be Warwick. Henry captured him at the Battle of Stoke in 1487 (the last battle of the Wars of the Roses) and put him to work in the palace kitchen, saying that he was too young to have given offence. The next impostor was a young man called Perkin Warbeck. He pretended to be Richard of York (Edward V's younger brother) and claimed that he had escaped from the Tower. Eventually Henry captured and executed him.

In his later years Henry VII became miserly and unpopular, but he remained shrewd, very hard-working and always knew when he could afford to be ruthless. When he died in 1509 there was no opposition to his son; he had founded the House of Tudor.

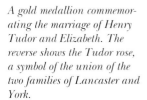

A gold medallion commemorating the marriage of Henry Tudor and Elizabeth. The reverse shows the Tudor rose, a symbol of the union of the two families of Lancaster and York.

THE ENGLISH ROYAL LINE OF SUCCESSION

❖

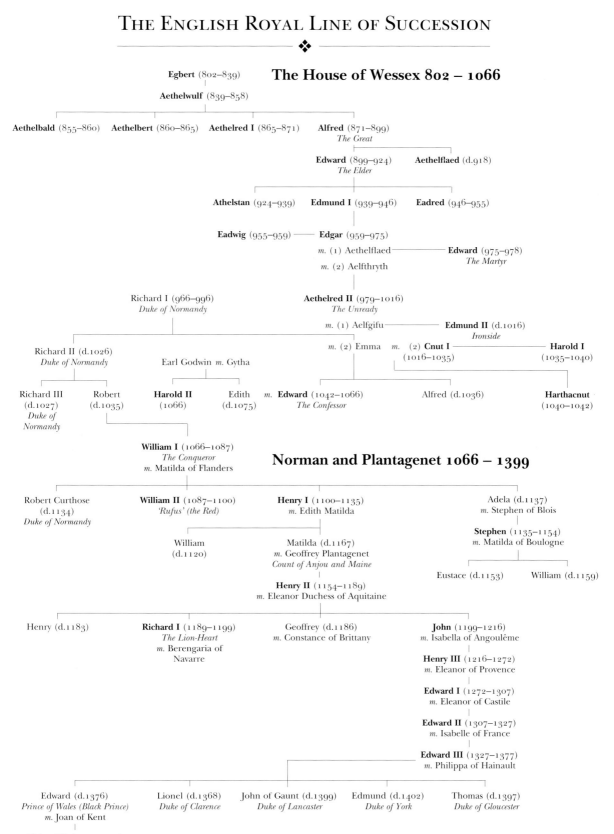

The House of Wessex 802 – 1066

Egbert (802–839)

Aethelwulf (839–858)

Aethelbald (855–860)   **Aethelbert** (860–865)   **Aethelred I** (865–871)   **Alfred** (871–899)
The Great

Edward (899–924)   **Aethelflaed** (d.918)
The Elder

Athelstan (924–939)   **Edmund I** (939–946)   **Eadred** (946–955)

Eadwig (955–959) — **Edgar** (959–975)

m. (1) Aethelflaed ———— **Edward** (975–978)
The Martyr

m. (2) Aelfthryth

Richard I (966–996)
Duke of Normandy

Aethelred II (979–1016)
The Unready

m. (1) Aelfgifu ———— **Edmund II** (d.1016)
Ironside

Richard II (d.1026)
Duke of Normandy

Earl Godwin *m.* Gytha

m. (2) Emma   *m.*   (2) **Cnut I** ———— **Harold I**
(1016–1035)   (1035–1040)

Richard III   Robert
(d.1027)   (d.1035)
Duke of
Normandy

Harold II
(1066)

Edith
(d.1075)

m. **Edward** (1042–1066)
The Confessor

Alfred (d.1036)

Harthacnut
(1040–1042)

William I (1066–1087)
The Conqueror
m. Matilda of Flanders

Norman and Plantagenet 1066 – 1399

Robert Curthose
(d.1134)
Duke of Normandy

William II (1087–1100)
'Rufus' (the Red)

Henry I (1100–1135)
m. Edith Matilda

Adela (d.1137)
m. Stephen of Blois

William
(d.1120)

Matilda (d.1167)
m. Geoffrey Plantagenet
Count of Anjou and Maine

Stephen (1135–1154)
m. Matilda of Boulogne

Eustace (d.1153)   William (d.1159)

Henry II (1154–1189)
m. Eleanor Duchess of Aquitaine

Henry (d.1183)

Richard I (1189–1199)
The Lion-Heart
m. Berengaria of
Navarre

Geoffrey (d.1186)
m. Constance of Brittany

John (1199–1216)
m. Isabella of Angoulême

Henry III (1216–1272)
m. Eleanor of Provence

Edward I (1272–1307)
m. Eleanor of Castile

Edward II (1307–1327)
m. Isabelle of France

Edward III (1327–1377)
m. Philippa of Hainault

Edward (d.1376)
Prince of Wales (Black Prince)
m. Joan of Kent

Lionel (d.1368)
Duke of Clarence

John of Gaunt (d.1399)
Duke of Lancaster

Edmund (d.1402)
Duke of York

Thomas (d.1397)
Duke of Gloucester

Richard II (1377–1399)

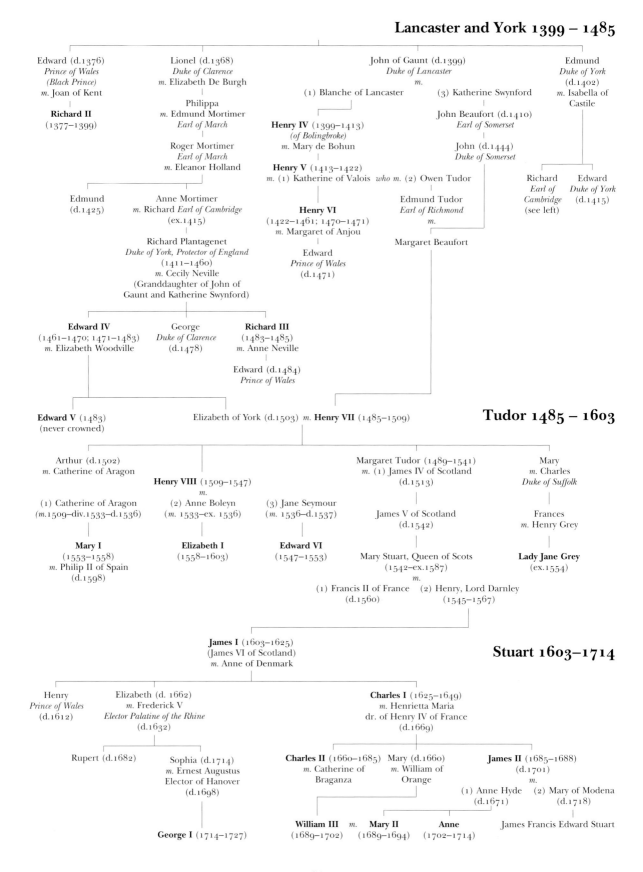

Hanoverian 1714 – 1901

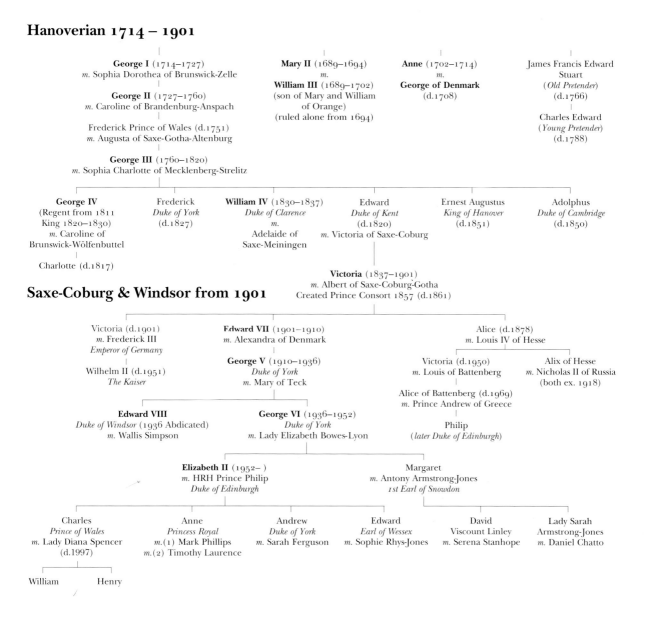

George I (1714–1727)
m. Sophia Dorothea of Brunswick-Zelle

George II (1727–1760)
m. Caroline of Brandenburg-Anspach

Frederick Prince of Wales (d.1751)
m. Augusta of Saxe-Gotha-Altenburg

George III (1760–1820)
m. Sophia Charlotte of Mecklenberg-Strelitz

Mary II (1689–1694)
m.
William III (1689–1702)
(son of Mary and William
of Orange)
(ruled alone from 1694)

Anne (1702–1714)
m.
George of Denmark
(d.1708)

James Francis Edward
Stuart
(*Old Pretender*)
(d.1766)

Charles Edward
(*Young Pretender*)
(d.1788)

George IV
(Regent from 1811
King 1820–1830)
m. Caroline of
Brunswick-Wölfenbuttel

Charlotte (d.1817)

Frederick
Duke of York
(d.1827)

William IV (1830–1837)
Duke of Clarence
m.
Adelaide of
Saxe-Meiningen

Edward
Duke of Kent
(d.1820)
m. Victoria of Saxe-Coburg

Ernest Augustus
King of Hanover
(d.1851)

Adolphus
Duke of Cambridge
(d.1850)

Victoria (1837–1901)
m. Albert of Saxe-Coburg-Gotha
Created Prince Consort 1857 (d.1861)

Saxe-Coburg & Windsor from 1901

Victoria (d.1901)
m. Frederick III
Emperor of Germany

Wilhelm II (d.1951)
The Kaiser

Edward VII (1901–1910)
m. Alexandra of Denmark

George V (1910–1936)
Duke of York
m. Mary of Teck

Alice (d.1878)
m. Louis IV of Hesse

Victoria (d.1950)
m. Louis of Battenberg

Alix of Hesse
m. Nicholas II of Russia
(both ex. 1918)

Alice of Battenberg (d.1969)
m. Prince Andrew of Greece

Edward VIII
Duke of Windsor (1936 Abdicated)
m. Wallis Simpson

George VI (1936–1952)
Duke of York
m. Lady Elizabeth Bowes-Lyon

Philip
(*later Duke of Edinburgh*)

Elizabeth II (1952–)
m. HRH Prince Philip
Duke of Edinburgh

Margaret
m. Antony Armstrong-Jones
1st Earl of Snowdon

Charles
Prince of Wales
m. Lady Diana Spencer
(d.1997)

Anne
Princess Royal
m.(1) Mark Phillips
m.(2) Timothy Laurence

Andrew
Duke of York
m. Sarah Ferguson

Edward
Earl of Wessex
m. Sophie Rhys-Jones

David
Viscount Linley
m. Serena Stanhope

Lady Sarah
Armstrong-Jones
m. Daniel Chatto

William   Henry

KINGS AND QUEENS OF SCOTLAND

❖

MAC ALPINE

843–58	Kenneth I
858–62	Donald I
862–77	Constantine I
877–78	Aedh
878–89	Eocha
889–900	Donald II
900–43	Constantine II
943–54	Malcolm I
954–62	Indulf
962–66	Duff
966–71	Colin
971–95	Kenneth II
995–97	Constantine III
997–1005	Kenneth III
1005–34	Malcolm II
1034–40	Duncan I
1040–57	Macbeth
1058	Luiach

CANMORE

1057–93	Malcolm III
1093	Donald Bane
1094	Duncan II
1094–97	Donald Bane
1097–1107	Edgar
1107–24	Alexander I
1124–53	David I
1153–65	Malcolm IV
1165–1214	William I
1214–49	Alexander II
1249–86	Alexander III
1286–90	Margaret
1290–92	No king

BALLIOL

1292–96	John Balliol
1296–1306	No king

BRUCE

1306–29	Robert I
1329–71	David II

STUART

1371–90	Robert II
1390–1406	Robert III
1406–19	Regent Albany
1419–24	Regent Murdoch
1424–37	James I
1437–60	James II
1460–88	James III
1488–1513	James IV
1513–42	James V
1542–67	Mary
1567–1625	JamesVI

In 1603 James VI became King of England, Wales and Ireland. From 1603 onwards the rulers of Scotland are the same as the rulers of England and Wales.

PRIME MINISTERS 1721–2001

❖

1721	Sir Robert Walpole
1741	Earl of Wilmington
1743	Henry Pelham
1754	Duke of Newcastle
1756	Duke of Devonshire
1757	Duke of Newcastle
1762	Earl of Bute
1763	George Grenville
1765	Marquess of Rockingham
1766	Earl of Chatham
1768	Duke of Grafton
1770	Lord North
1782	Marquess of Rockingham
1782	Earl of Shelburne
1783	Duke of Portland
1783	William Pitt
1801	Henry Addington
1804	William Pitt
1806	William Wyndham Grenville
1807	Duke of Portland
1809	Spencer Perceval
1812	Earl of Liverpool
1827	George Canning
1827	Viscount Goderich
1828	Duke of Wellington
1830	Earl Grey

1834	Viscount Melbourne
1834	Duke of Wellington
1834	Sir Robert Peel
1835	Viscount Melbourne
1841	Sir Robert Peel
1846	Lord John Russell
1852	Earl of Derby
1852	Earl of Aberdeen
1855	Viscount Palmerston
1858	Earl of Derby
1859	Viscount Palmerston
1865	Earl Russell
1866	Earl of Derby
1868	Benjamin Disraeli
1868	William Ewart Gladstone
1874	Benjamin Disraeli
1880	William Ewart Gladstone
1885	Marquess of Salisbury
1886	William Ewart Gladstone
1886	Marquess of Salisbury
1892	William Ewart Gladstone
1894	Earl of Rosebery
1895	Marquess of Salisbury
1902	Arthur James Balfour
1905	Sir Henry Campbell-Bannerman

1908	Herbert Henry Asquith
1916	David Lloyd George
1922	Andrew Bonar Law
1923	Stanley Baldwin
1924	James Ramsay MacDonald
1924	Stanley Baldwin
1929	James Ramsay MacDonald
1935	Stanley Baldwin
1937	Neville Chamberlain
1940	Winston Churchill
1945	Clement Attlee
1951	Winston Churchill
1955	Sir Anthony Eden
1957	Harold Macmillan
1963	Sir Alec Douglas-Home
1964	Harold Wilson
1970	Edward Heath
1974	Harold Wilson
1976	James Callaghan
1979	Margaret Thatcher
1990	John Major
1997	Tony Blair

INDEX

❖

Acknowledgements

❖

p6 BL (Ms.Claud. B iv, f 24v); p7 BM; p8r Ashmolean Museum, Oxford; p9 BL (Ms.Cott.Claud.B iv, f59); p10tl BM, r CCC, Cambridge (Ms.183); p10br CCC, Cambridge; p11 BL (Ms.Cott.Tib. B i, f140v); p12b Historic Scotland; p16 BL (Ms.Stowe 944, f6); pp17-19 Michael Holford; p20t BL (seal of William I), b BL (Ms.Roy.16 F ii, f73); p21 ET; p22 House of Commons Education Unit; p23t CCC, Oxford (CCC MC 157), b CCC, Cambridge (Ms 373, f95v); p25b Pictor International; p26 BL (Ms.Roy.10 E iv, f65v); Bibliothèque Nationale de France (Ms.Fr.2829, f18); p28 CCC, Cambridge (Ms.16, f44v); p29 BL (Ms.Ad.46144); p30 ET; p31 BL (Ms.Cott.Nero. D ii, f177); p33 CCC, Cambridge (Ms.10, f181); p34 BL (Ms.Add.42130); p35 BL (Ms.Cott. Claud. B ii, f341); p36t BL (Ms. Harl.2278, f100v), bl & br Michael Holford; p37t BL (Ms Harl.4866, f88), bl ET, br Irish Tourist Board; p38 BL (Ms.Add.42130, f187); p39 Michael Jenner; p40t CCC, Cambridge (Ms16, f66v), b Michael Jenner; p41 Mirror Syndication/BTA; p42 Michael Jenner; p43 BL (Ms.Cott.Nero D ii, f183v); p44-5 BL (Ms.Cott.Tib. B v, f5); p45t EH; p47t BL (Ms. Cott.Tib. B v, f7), b Bodleian Library, Oxford (Ms. Maps. Notts.a.2); p48t Bridgeman Art Library, b Michael Jenner; p49cl & bl BM; p50t BL (Ms.Stowe 17, f89v), b BL (Ms. Add. 42130, f181); p51t (Ms.Roy.10E iv, f19), c BL (Ms. Add. 42130, f193); b BL Claude B1VF67; p53t Bibliothèque Royale Albert 1er, Brussels (BR 13076.77, f24), b Cambridge University Aerial Photography Unit; p54 Bridgeman; p55 Michael Jenner; p56 BL (Ms. Add.42130, f147v); p57t BL (Cott.Claud.b IV, f24v), b Winchester Cathedral; p58t BL (Ms.Roy. 14C vii, f136); p58-9b Cadw; p59t (Ms. Cott.Nero.D ii, f177); p60t Nat. Museum of Ireland; p61 Mirror Syndication/BTA; p62t BL (Ms.Add.24153, f125v); p62-3b Historic Scotland; p63cl BM, br Dean & Chapter of Westminster; p64 Royal Collection © HM the Queen; p65b BL (Cott.Ch.xix.4); p66cl BL (Ms. Roy.13Bviii, f26), b Bodleian Library, Oxford (Ms.Laud.Misc.720, f226); pp67 Bridgeman; p68 BL (Ms.Cott. Nero.Dvi, f61v); p70 BL (Ms.Eg. 1065,f9); p71 Bridgeman; p72t & b BL (Ms.Add.42130); p74t Bridgeman, b BL; p75t Oxford Picture Library, b BL (Ms.Sloane 1977, f7); p76 Michael Holford; p77 Fitzwilliam Museum, Cambridge; p78 Christ Church, Oxford (Ms.92, f4v); p79 Bibliothèque Nationale de France (Ms.Fr.2643 f97v); p80t BL (Ms.Add.42130, f161v), b BL (Ms. Roy.20Cvii, f41v); pp81, 83 Bridgeman; p84 Dean & Chapter of Westminster Abbey; p86t BL (Ms.Harl.1319, f41v), b EH; p87 W&N; p88 Bibliothèque Nationale de France (Ms.fr.5054); p89 Royal Collection © HM The Queen; p91 Universiteitsbibliotheek, Gent; p92 BM;

All maps are by Hardlines, Charlbury, Oxfordshire.

Abbreviations:
BL = British Library; BM = British Museum; CCC = Corpus Christi College; EH = English Heritage; ET = E. T. Archive; IWM = Imperial War Museum; NG = National Gallery, London; NPG = National Portrait Gallery, London; V & A = Victoria & Albert Museum, London; W & N = Weidenfeld & Nicolson Archives